COLUMBIA COLLEGE

W9-DHU-837

ON THE POETRY OF

Mark Twain

LIBRARY
OF
COLUMBIA COLLEGE
CHICAGO, ILLINOIS

WITH SELECTIONS

FROM HIS VERSE &

& ARTHUR L. SCOTT

UNIVERSITY OF ILLINOIS PRESS

URBANA AND LONDON, 1966 &

Clemens, Samuel Langhorne
"

© 1966 by the Board of Trustees of the University of Illinois. Manufactured in the United States of America. Library of Congress Catalog Card No. 66-10344.

811.4
T9690

6026

For my father ❧

⤸ A Foreword

Let no one mistake this book as an effort to establish a reputation for Mark Twain in the realm of poetry. It is no such thing. Nor is it a critical study of Mark Twain's poetry. It is, rather, a survey of the life-long interest of Mark Twain in poetry — a form of writing which almost everyone thinks he detested.

For over a decade, as a pleasant sideline, I have been copying down pieces of verse by Mark Twain wherever I found them and taking notes on his comments about poets and poetry. My research in the Mark Twain Papers at Berkeley several years ago uncovered so many new poems that my interest came to a head. Here were scores of additional poems which no one had ever mentioned, much less printed.

The Mark Twain Company has allowed me to quote freely in my text from these unpublished poems and to print for the first time a number of these manuscripts in their entirety. The sensitive reader in search of inspired or meticulously polished gems of verse will be disappointed. He will come to realize, indeed, that the Muse of formal poetry held Mark Twain at arm's length, as a rule, except when his mood was humorous.

The best of Mark Twain's descriptive and serious poetry, therefore, is still to be found in the magnificent prose passages of *A Tramp Abroad, Life on the Mississippi, Huckleberry Finn,* and other books. The challenge of composing serious poetry seemed to make Mark Twain self-conscious, to cramp his style, and frequently to curb his inspiration. A "divine amateur," perhaps, in his prose, Mark Twain was most often simply an amateur in his verse.

He was, however, an amateur in the true sense. From his boyhood until his death, as I try to show, he *loved* poetry. If he did not write it well, he did not try very hard, either. He hated to revise. Much of it was dashed off just as you and I might dash off some lines for an office party or a child's memory book. Other poems were merely stuffed into newspaper columns or whipped up to lend variety to some prose piece. Of his later poems — longer and sadder — few were penned with any thought other than to assuage his private grief.

My particular thanks go to Henry Nash Smith and Frederick Anderson of the University of California for friendly assistance with the Mark Twain Papers; to Burney Fishback and the Mark Twain Research Foundation of Perry, Missouri, for their friendship and for a rare copy of the 1871 "Ballotd" broadside; to Mrs. Edith C. Salsbury of the Mark Twain Memorial, Hartford, for sending me several new poems; to the Yale University Library for a microfilm of Mark Twain's Scrapbook; to the Buffalo Public Library for a microfilm of the Buffalo *Express* files for 1869-71; to the cooperative staff of the University of Illinois Library; to numerous libraries throughout the country which have been most generous with interlibrary loans over the years; and to the Huntington Library of San Marino, California, a congenial, inspiring, and beautiful research center.

Finally, as usual, I thank my wife — as patient and accurate a proofreader as any scholar can wish.

List of Poems ❧

Early in 1951 in Hollywood, California, an auctioneer sold for $750 the manuscript of what was advertised as the "Only Known POEM by Mark Twain."[1] Seldom has a manuscript been so grossly misrepresented.

ट॰ॐ ट॰ॐ ट॰ॐ

*A*bout 1874 Mark Twain jotted several notes on the back of a tiny envelope. One of these notes is well known: "I like history, biography, travels, curious facts and strange happenings, and science. And I detest novels, poetry, and theology."[2] Mark Twain's official biographer gave prominence to this "literary declaration"[3] and succeeding biographers have seized happily upon the forthright statement.

This is unfortunate. We know from many sources that all his life Mark Twain did love to read history, biography, and curious facts. Similar evidence is needed to prove the case *against* novels, poetry, and theology. Little can be found. His late writings — many of them only now trickling into print — show that theology was much on his mind. In a way he actually loved the study of God. The aim of this book is to reveal that he also loved poetry. It is time that we stop judging the literary taste of a volatile man like Mark Twain by a thought hurriedly scrawled near the start of his professional career.

[1] The auction ad is in the Mark Twain Papers (MTP) in the General Library of the University of California, Berkeley. So is the UP release of April 11, 1951, as it appeared in the Berkeley *Gazette*. The poem was "In Memoriam" (1897).
[2] MTP, Paine #277.
[3] Albert Bigelow Paine, *Mark Twain: A Biography* (New York, 1912), 512.

First let us take a glance at the general impression most people have of Mark Twain's interest in poetry. In his boyhood, we may remember, he wrote both sentimental and comic verses for the newspapers. In *Roughing It* he has that long spoof called "The Aged Pilot Man." If we do not recall the children's song in *Joan of Arc,* we surely recall the Duke's "Shakespearean" soliloquy in *Huckleberry Finn,* as well as the obituary verse of Emmeline Grangerford. The heartfelt poetry he wrote on the death of his daughter is remembered. Some may call to mind that his travel books contain a light verse or two and a few translations. Beyond this it has also been impressed on us by the biographers that Mark Twain was inordinately fond of a few particular poems and poets.

If this summary is correct, it will surprise most people to hear that in 1935 Mark Twain's bibliographer devoted a special section to Poems and Translations. He listed 28 original poems by Mark Twain.[4] Today at least 45 additional poems by Mark Twain are in print and more than 50 others are in manuscript form. This means that well over 120 poems were written by the man who "detested poetry." As time goes on, still more of his verses will be turned up in private letters and in musty files. Already we have enough evidence, however, to make a sane evaluation.

At the outset a few statistics might help. Of the poems I know, 95 are comic, 31 are serious. Of the comic poetry, 85 per cent was written before 1890, whereas most of the serious poetry was written after that date. After 1890, when life began to sour on him, Mark Twain composed three times as much serious poetry as he did comic. In general, his serious poems also have longer lines and more lines. Half of his comic poems are of 10 lines or less; only two are over 50 lines. On the other hand, only one-third of his serious poems are of 10 lines or less, while eight are over 50 lines. As a result, his smaller number of serious poems runs to nearly 1,500 lines, compared to about 1,600 lines for the comic poems. The implication is obvious: metrical jokes lacked the sustaining power of deeper emotions.

Mark Twain's daughter recalled recently the discussions her family used to have about literature. "Very often," she said, "these discussions came around to a subject Father had fun talking about — poetry, and whether people should write poetry or not."[5] Probably he was unaware of how much poetry he himself had written through the years. Edward Wagenknecht considers it a "wonderful thing that he should have been able to do it at all."[6] Wagenknecht mentions four poems in passing.

[4] Merle Johnson, *A Bibliography of Mark Twain* (New York, 1935), 135-139.
[5] Clara Clemens Samossoud, "His Daughter Remembers," *Saturday Review,* Vol. 43, Part II, p. 24 (July 25, 1960).
[6] *Mark Twain: The Man and His Work* (New Haven, 1935), 77.

More recently, DeLancey Ferguson has shown still less interest in Mark Twain's verse, although he is shrewd to observe that Mark Twain's avowed dislike of poetry was far from absolute: "His use of them for purposes of parody and burlesque shows that he had read most of the standard popular poets of his day."[7]

Closer than other critics to understanding Mark Twain's style, Gladys Bellamy believes that the ear was his most receptive organ. "His sense of sound," she says, "was as delicately attuned, perhaps, as that of Poe. . . ."[8] The excellence of his style, moreover, she attributes in part to its long rhythms, its vivid vocabulary, "and an imagery in intimate accord with the senses."[9]

A style such as this is adaptable to poetry. At least one person in his own day recognized this, and Mark Twain must have been flattered for he saved the tribute. It is an interesting little article, which shows how the writing of poetry and prose has been combined in men like Emerson, Holmes, Stevenson, and Kipling. The insight, fancy, verbal feeling of their prose, says the writer, suggest their poetic ability, when added to a sense of rhythm. He continues: "There is one American writer today whose diffidence about putting his thoughts into meter may mean a heavy loss to American literature. The prose of Mark Twain shows the presence of all the faculties that go to make up a poet in such brilliancy that his failure to exercise them in that way can be regarded as a misfortune."[10]

That Mark Twain did exercise these faculties in that way is the subject here. Let's start at the beginning. As for juvenilia, who knows what Mark Twain may have written in school or in all the newspapers he worked for as a boy and young man? Vying for poetry by local people, the newspapers fostered a poetry vogue in the 1850's. Minnie Brashear is likely correct in believing that during the early 1850's young Sam Clemens "had a verse-writing period which he probably kept secret, and which he did not think enough of to record in his biography further than to acknowledge satirically three attempts."[11] Typical of these early poems are "The Heart's Lament: To Bettie W———e, of Tennessee"* and the

---

[7] *Mark Twain: Man and Legend* (Indianapolis, 1943), 206-207.
[8] *Mark Twain as a Literary Artist* (Norman, Okla., 1950), 187.
[9] Ibid., 265.
[10] MTP, Clippings file, Kansas City *Star,* October 7, 1900. A pencil note in the margin says, "Mr. Clemens — Pardon the intrusion, but why don't you? Henry J. Haskell." The piece is entitled " 'Mark Twain' as a Poet."
[11] *Mark Twain, Son of Missouri* (Chapel Hill, N.C., 1934), 145.
* An asterisk following the title of a poem indicates that the complete poem appears elsewhere in this volume.

better-known (because of its title) "Love Concealed: To Miss Katie of H——l"*. These were not humorous, but were products of the current vogue. Young Sam, then about seventeen, wanted to be published, so he took the simplest way. Besides, as a sentimental young apprentice he loved to print favorite poems on scraps of cotton or silk for his girl friends.[12]

These early poems display the popular conventions of poetic diction, alliteration, inverted word order, amorous clichés, a jingling meter, and a kind of wistful teariness. If composing verse like this had any effect upon the boy, it was probably to enlarge his vocabulary, to improve his ear for sounds and rhythms, to help him to think in terms of images, and to imbue him with a contempt for artificial sentiment. This contempt endured.

That Mark Twain began to react against sentimentalism even while purveying it himself is shown by two quatrains of the early 1850's and by one long satire. Forerunner of the mortuary verse of Emmeline Grangerford is

> Weep stranger, for a father spilled
> From a stage-coach, and thereby killed:
> His name John Sykes, a maker of sassengers
> Slain with three other outside passengers.[13]

And river-brag swells the resolutions of a desperate young man whose girl has slighted him:

> I'll flog the *Young Earthquake,*
>   The earth I will physic
> Volcanoes I'll strangle,
> Or choke with the phthisic.[14]

The satire is "The Burial of Sir Abner Gilstrap" (24 lines)*, an attack on a rival newspaper editor. It concludes on a note characteristic of Mark Twain's later style.

> No useless coffin confined his breast,
>   Nor in sheet nor in shirt we bound him;
> But he lay like an Editor taking his rest,
>   With a Hannibal Journal round him.[15]

The fun of writing lines like these seems to have killed the boy's sentimentalism even before he embarked on his Wanderjahr in 1853 at the age of seventeen. The next fifteen months are poorly documented, but Paine believes that Mark Twain contributed a great deal of burlesque

[12] See Dixon Wecter, *Sam Clemens of Hannibal* (Boston, 1952), 210. For a listing of these early poems see Edgar M. Branch, "A Chronological Bibliography of the Writings of Samuel Clemens to June 8, 1867," *American Literaure,* XVIII, 109-159 (May, 1946).
[13] Wecter, *Sam Clemens of Hannibal,* 246.
[14] Brashear, *Mark Twain,* 146.
[15] Ibid., 138-139.

obituary verse to the Philadelphia *Ledger*.[16] Except for some nonsense lines in his "Snodgrass" letters,[17] however, only one poem has turned up to represent these typesetting years of mid-1853 to 1857. This poem, "The Storm" (16 lines), is part of a humorous sketch, presumably written in Philadelphia in 1854. The first stanza will serve to give the flavor of its deliberate banality, clichés, and anticlimax:

> Just see the lightning's lurid glare!
> Just hear the thunder's crash!
> Behold that riven stable there: —
> Oh, what an awful smash![18]

During the next four years, 1857-61, Mark Twain was on the river. He read Shakespeare and Milton, he says, but he seems to have been too busy piloting to produce poetry.

Not until 1864 did Mark Twain turn again to versifying. In his letters home he had fun combining lines from different poems and adding absurd conclusions to well-known stanzas. This showed, at least, some reading. He also developed a contemplative, poetic nature which few of his associates saw. Thus, the stately "Burial of Moses" by C. F. Alexander made an immense impression on him. He copied it in his notebook, memorized it, used to recite it with great power all his life. The noble phrasing and majestic imagery of the poem may have influenced his own style, which was in a formative stage. "Samuel Clemens was still in the classroom," says Paine. "Everything came as a lesson. . . . The poetic phase of things particularly impressed him."[19]

Impressed though he was, Mark Twain did not try his own hand at this sort of poetry. Not yet — not for thirty years more. Instead, in 1864 he sought to regale his Western audience with a long parody on romantic poetry. "The Aged Pilot Man" (137 lines)* was written for the Virginia City *Occidental,* which died before publishing it; so it was carelessly stuffed into *Roughing It* eight years later.[20] The poem will be remembered as the gusty narrative about "a dreadful storm" on the Erie Canal. Modest in its pretensions, the poem is a success. The language has vigor. The form is sure and the ridicule incisive. "The Aged Pilot Man" is the most elaborate example in verse form of Mark Twain's contempt as a young man for all emotions which are absurdly out of proportion to the true circumstances.

[16] Paine, *Biography,* 98.
[17] Edgar M. Branch, *The Literary Apprenticeship of Mark Twain* (Urbana, Ill., 1950), 224.
[18] MTP, DW #12, unpublished typescript. © Copyright 1966 by the Mark Twain Company.
[19] *Biography,* 218.
[20] Branch, *Literary Apprenticeship,* 278.

The writing of this poem, perhaps, renewed Mark Twain's interest in rhyming. Having written almost no verse for a decade, he now composed upwards of a dozen poems during the next two years, 1865-66. By this time he had left Nevada and was living in California. These were mostly light poems designed to spruce up his newspaper letters; they average about 24 lines. Different types of light verse represent these years. "A Rich Epigram" (18 lines)* chided a bellicose theatre manager for assaulting one of his actors.[21] The actor sued Maguire for $5,000, whereon Mark Twain switched sides with "Nursery Rhyme" (26 lines)*:

> Macdougall, d——n your eyes!
> Don't legal quips devise. . . .[22]

A small cut above this timely doggerel, which was dashed off to meet a copy deadline, is "He Done His Level Best" (24 lines)*. Mark Twain liked this well enough to preserve it in *Sketches New and Old* (1875). The old swinging gusto is still here, plus vivid characterization of an Arkansas circuit-rider.[23]

Unless a local event stirred his Muse, Mark Twain's forays into verse at this time were chiefly for parody. Being a lazy man in some respects, he liked having a ready-made meter and he liked the ease of carrying over whole lines or phrases from the original. He drew upon a boyhood favorite in writing "The Mysterious Chinaman" (23 lines)*:

> Once upon a morning dreary, while I pondered, weak and weary,
> Over many a quaint and curious shirt that me and Steve has
> wore. . . .[24]

Happy nonsense, all of it.

Mark Twain's newspaper correspondence from Hawaii in 1866 shows his reversion to the sport of combining alternate lines from two poems. "The Burial of Sir John Moore" and "The Destruction of Sennacherib" fuse into a curious ballad (28 lines)*. It opens:

> The Assyrian came down like a wolf on the fold,
>   The turf with our bayonets turning,
> And his cohorts were gleaming in purple and gold,
>   And our lanterns dimly burning.[25]

Mark Twain says that he recited this poem to Mr. Brown, his seasick

[21] Mark Twain's Scrapbook, courtesy of the Yale University Library. A slightly different version appears in Paine, *Biography*, 275-276.
[22] Ibid. The spelling of the actor's name has changed.
[23] *Sketches New and Old*, The Works of Mark Twain, Definitive Edition, ed. Albert B. Paine (New York, 1922), VII, 71-72.
[24] Written for "M. E. G's Album," printed in *The Twainian*, p. 3 (July-August, 1947). A photostat is in MTP. Steve Gillis was his roommate in San Francisco. As for Poe, Mark Twain used to carry his poetry around with him during his Keokuk days in the mid-1850's.
[25] Walter F. Frear, *Mark Twain and Hawaii* (Chicago, 1947), 411-412.

companion, who thereupon threw up everything he had eaten for the last three days.

At this time Mark Twain also took to making fun of sentimental love poetry. Annoyed at the "cheap climax" of a poem called "My Kingdom" by Paul Duoir, he wrote a line-by-line burlesque of the first four stanzas. "My Ranch" (16 lines)* is not side-splitting. Where Duoir wrote of his "queen" ("Her will is mine, and all my toil her gain"), Mark Twain wrote of his sow ("Her swill is mine, and all my slops her gain").[26]

More interesting than the other nonsense of these final Western years, 1865-66, are two serious poems. "Sparkling and Bright" (20 lines) found its way into his notebook during the peaceful voyage home from Hawaii. Although he closed it with a stupid quatrain about the stench of the natives, the rest of the piece proves that he was coming to understand the advantages of verse for creating certain moods:

> Floating away, like a fountain's spray
> Or the snowwhite plume of a maiden
> The Smoke-wreaths rise to the starlit skies
> With blissful fragrance laden.
>
> Then smoke away till golden ray
> Lights in the dawn of the morrow
> For a cheerful cigar like a shield will bar
> The heart from care & sorrow.[27]

These lines of rather conventional sentiment are less surprising than a poem which Mark Twain incorporated into one of his newspaper letters from Hawaii in 1866. "Polonius' Advice to His Son — Paraphrased from Hamlet" (28 lines)* is an earnest adaptation of the soliloquy to a popular Victorian stanza, complete with rhyme. Although the poem is set in a silly context in the letter, it appears to be something he really worked over.[28] Mark Twain could have been engaged in vainer pursuits than this verbal exercise. One is reminded of the way another young newspaper man, Ben Franklin, set about to perfect *his* literary style.

In his newspaper and magazine columns Mark Twain sometimes printed his own verse under the guise that it was the work of someone else. This makes our research more tricky. Such a poem was "Miss Slim-

[26] *Sketches of the Sixties by Bret Harte and Mark Twain,* ed. John Howell (San Francisco, 1926), 188-190. This appeared first in *The Californian,* October 28, 1865.
[27] These opening lines, with half a dozen changes, are printed in *Mark Twain's Notebook,* ed. Albert B. Paine (New York, 1935), 29. The original notebooks and later typescripts are in MTP. Hereafter, all references will be to the latter, whose pages are numbered. This poem appears in Notebook #4-5 (III), p. 38. Mark Twain may have borrowed his title and meter from Charles Fenno Hoffman's *carpe diem* poem, which he'd have liked.
[28] Frear, *Mark Twain and Hawaii,* 367-368.

mens" (32 lines)*, which he composed to vent his feelings about a frightful gossip on board ship. His newspaper letter reports that for New Year's Day "one of the boys in the after cabin served her up to the tune of 'Auld Lang Syne'. . . .There were eight verses of home-spun doggerel."[29] The "one of the boys in the after cabin" was Mark Twain himself. All eight verses of the poem (with editing) appear in his pocket notebook of the period.

Two months later, while visiting his family in Missouri, he made a similar pretense regarding the authorship of a suicide poem which begins: "In sorrow I sorrow, O sorrowful day!"* In this case external evidence is hardly needed to identify the author.[30]

Perhaps composed at a later date, but treating a Western theme, is the 44-line "Miner's Lament"* in which a lonely and unsuccessful miner thinks wistfully of "the good old times" with tasty food, unpatched clothes, and a "gentle love" so far away.[31]

We are up to 1867 now, the year Mark Twain made the first of his many trips to Europe. During the two years just past, he had rediscovered the joy of writing poetry, as a young man sometimes rediscovers the girl next door. He had learned, also, that poetry was useful for other things than comic obituaries and amorous laments. From this time on, scarcely a year went by when he failed to write a poem or two, sometimes half a dozen. When his comic Muse forsook him in the 1890's, his verse lost its laughter. But it continued to flow, as if writing verse had become a compulsion.

His private notebooks, too, from now until his death attest the power of certain poetic lines to mesmerize him. Time and again he made these three short entries:

> Better lo'ed you'll never be,
> And will you no come back again?

> Sing me the songs that I once loved to hear, long, long ago.
> Whisper the names that to me were so dear.

> In the days when we went gipsying, a long time ago.

This last, in particular, seemed to haunt him, so often did he write it

[29] Three stanzas are reprinted in *Mark Twain's Travels with Mr. Brown,* ed. Franklin Walker and G. Ezra Dane (New York, 1940), 63-64. A fourth stanza appears in *Mark Twain's Notebook,* 44.

[30] *The Missouri Democrat,* March 12-13, 1867. Reprinted in *Mark Twain: Life as I Find It,* ed. Charles Neider (Garden City, N.Y., 1961), 14.

[31] For this poem (an unidentified newspaper clipping in Mark Twain's name) I am indebted to Mrs. Edith C. Salsbury, Chairman of the Research Committee, Mark Twain Memorial, Hartford.

down. His favorite stanza from Holmes's "Last Leaf" also appears over and over again:

> The mossy marbles rest
> On the lips that he has pressed
> In their bloom;
> And the names he loved to hear
> Have been carved for many a year
> On the tomb.

He did not always get the words right and, in later years, he sometimes substituted "we" for "he," but the nostalgic sadness of this and other poems had a potent appeal for Mark Twain even in his formative years.

A like sadness animates the poem which he wrote on shipboard later this same year of 1867. Near the end of the Mediterranean cruise, the genteel Mrs. S. L. Severance begged him to write something sober for a magazine like *The Atlantic Monthly*. The next day he handed her the 60-line poem "Good Bye"*, which he read at the farewell assembly. In the poem he compares the passengers to ships whose courses will soon carry them apart:

> Some shall be famed in many lands
> As good ships, fast and fair,
> And some shall strangely disappear,
> Men know not when or where.[32]

Conventional though this is, it nevertheless displays a swinging meter, an ear for sound, an apt basic image, and a keen sense of human destiny. The rhetoric, indeed, is somewhat better than one might expect of a frisky young humorist during his final day at sea. It is amazing that he took the time to write any sort of poem.

As far as I know, this was Mark Twain's last effort (except for "A Ballotd," 1871) to write serious poetry until personal tragedies began to afflict him in the 1890's. During the happy interim of twenty-five years, he seems to have written about three dozen poems, a low average for him. They were all for laughs. The first two were also shipboard poems: "Ye Equinoctial Storm" (32 lines)* and "Tropic Chidings" (24 lines)*. Although written in 1868, they did not see print until someone sent them to the San Francisco *Wasp* in 1884.[33] The first, like "Miss Slimmens," dealt with specific acquaintances and was also to be sung to the tune of "Auld Lang Syne." The second was a silly He-She dialogue.

That same year, while living in Washington, D.C., Mark Twain

---

[32] First printed by Mrs. Severance in the Cleveland *Plain Dealer,* April 27, 1910, the week of Mark Twain's death. Reprinted in *The Twainian,* pp. 1-2 (June, 1945). Paine quotes eight lines in *Biography,* 341.

[33] Reprinted in *The Twainian,* p. 4 (July-August, 1946).

whipped his Muse into mock fury against one Alexander M. C. Ball, a harness maker in Elizabeth, New Jersey. Ball was claiming authorship of the popular "Rock Me to Sleep, Mother." In support of his *own* claim, Mark Twain wrote a poem called "Rock Him to Sleep" (18 lines)*. He longed to dry up Ball's "stale, oozy fount of ineffable bosh." In this poem, said Mark Twain, "I will furnish my evidence, and at the same time I will destroy this Ball."[34] While in Washington he also amused himself attacking the poetry written by congressmen. He even submitted an all-purpose verse of his own to replace everything after stanza three of all congressional poems.[35]

While conducting the humor department of the new *Galaxy* magazine during 1870-71, Mark Twain returned zestfully to his attack on what he called "post-mortem poetry." "There is an element about some poetry," he maintained, "which is able to make even physical suffering and death cheerful things to contemplate and consummations to be desired."[36] It was his practice to print mortuary verse sent to him by "correspondents." Some of the verse satirized, however, is choice enough to make us suspect its authorship.

Next he had fun in breaking down a warranty deed into short lines and arranging it in stanzas to resemble poetry. He called it "The Story of a Gallant Deed" (45 lines)* and its meter is supposed to be roughly that of *Hiawatha*.[37] The following month, in order to demonstrate Homer's love for "political economy," Mark Twain purported to cite Book IX of the *Iliad:*

> Fiat justitia, ruat coelum,
> Post mortem unum, ante bellum,
> Hic jacet hoc, ex-parte res,
> Politicum, e-conomico est.[38]

The most entertaining poem of this 1868-71 period is "Three Aces: Jim Todd's Episode in Social Euchre" (32 lines)*. This dialect poem in the fashion of Bret Harte's "Heathen Chinee" appeared in the Buffalo *Express* on December 3, 1870. It is told by a man who had been tricked into betting on the top three cards of his hand. He was sure that he had an unbeatable three aces. He found, however, that they lost to three ordinary clubs — a flush! And Mark Twain probably used the same nom

[34] First printed in the Cincinnati *Evening Chronicle* in Mark Twain's letter from Washington, March 4, 1868. Reprinted in *The Twainian*, pp. 2-3 (February, 1943).
[35] See the *Mark Twain Quarterly*, V, 3, 5 (Summer, 1942), for comments on Mark Twain's piece "Congressional Poetry."
[36] *The Galaxy*, IX, 864-865 (June, 1870).
[37] Ibid., X, 287 (August, 1870).
[38] Ibid., X, 425 (September, 1870).

de plume "Carl Byng" when he wrote the delightful "Review of Holiday Literature" for the Christmas Eve edition of 1870. This detailed analysis of a Mother Goose rhyme is a happy spoof of what later came to be called the New Criticism.[39]

There is good reason to believe that more than a dozen additional poems appearing in the *Express* during Mark Twain's editorship in 1869-70 were actually his, although most of them appeared either anonymously or under such names as "Somefellow," "Mark Lemon," "Hi Slocum," or "Ab O'Riginee"*. Several, such as "Three Aces," have been identified by long-time Twainians; others have been lately dug out and mentioned by Henry Duskis in *The Forgotten Writings of Mark Twain* (New York, 1963). These poems, totaling almost 300 lines, are all comic or satirical. Their merit is about what might be expected.

Even before moving to Hartford in the fall of 1871 Mark Twain displayed his lively interest in Connecticut politics by composing a large broadside:

A BALLOTD.
OWED PHOR THE TYMZ; not the knusepaper.
By TWARK MAIN, Skulemarster.*[40]

He dated it "Harfford Sitteigh, Meigh the Sicksteanth, 1871." It is a political satire and, at 368 lines, by far the longest poem he ever wrote. Despite its fantastic spelling, "A Ballotd" is not nonsense of the "Three Aces" type. It is a serious poem in the cast of Lowell's more trenchant *Biglow Papers,* the second series of which had appeared in book form only four years earlier.

Two-thirds of the poem describes a gubernatorial election in which the Democrats, whose man was backed by Boss Tweed and Tammany, stuffed the New Haven ballot boxes and destroyed Republican ballots. The final third outlines the honorable past of the Democratic Party in the days of Jefferson and Jackson, then attacks the more recent "dejenerait Demokrats."

Mark Twain may have been inconsistent in his misspellings, but there was nothing shaky or uncertain about his wrath. As for the vice during the recent election, he professed to take comfort in the fact that

---

[39] Both the poem and the review appeared over the signature of "Carl Byng" and Mark Twain repeatedly denied that it was his poem or his nom de plume. He was co-owner and editor of the paper at this time and there are cogent reasons to ignore his denials. See my "Review of Holiday Literature," *College English,* XXIII, 385-387 (February, 1962). See also a full discussion of this nom de plume in Margaret Duckett, *Mark Twain and Bret Harte* (Norman, Okla., 1964), Chapter 4.

[40] Johnson, *Bibliography,* 132, misspells "Ballotd" and says there are only 48 lines of verse. For my photostat I am grateful to Burney Fishback and the Mark Twain Research Foundation, Perry, Mo.

The parteigh's dedd that praktised it,
    It dyde the other da;
  It kild itselph, by nursing frawd,
    It thru itselph awa.

Also at about this time Mark Twain tried to make an absurd parody of "The Old Oaken Bucket," starting: "How sick to my soul are the scenes of my beer-hood."[41] Then, two weeks after Christmas he opened his checkbook and was promptly moved to write "Those Annual Bills" (12 lines)*, a parody on "Those Evening Bells" by Thomas Moore.[42]

Mark Twain's second-longest poem of this carefree quarter-century was "New Cock Robin" (76 lines)*. This was a light-hearted satire on four men who in 1872 aspired to succeed Horace Greeley as editor of the New York *Tribune*. Whitelaw Reid (the winner) and Speaker Blaine set forth their qualifications at some length. Schuyler Colfax and George William Curtis were more concise, perhaps because rhymes for their names were less abundant. Verbal ingenuity was part of the fun: rain, reign, rein; fain, feign, fane. At the end Mark Twain said he could not present his own qualifications, because he had run out of rhymes for his name:

  The recondite Radical Rep. from Chill Maine
  O, bothering, troublesome, itching chil-Blaine —
  Has used all the words except vain and insane
  That happily rhyme with Yours Truly, Mark Twain.

Apparently the poem was well received, for the Chicago *Tribune* of January 2, 1873, copied it from the Hartford *Evening Post*.[43]

How forgetful Mark Twain could be, even in the 1870's, is shown by the circumstances behind a little poem he wrote only six years later. He had just attended a party where a poem had been read in which every line rhymed with the name of one of the guests. "I mean to borrow and use that idea someday," he wrote in his notebook,[44] forgetting his "New Cock Robin." So in January, 1879, he entered some doggerel (16 lines) beginning:

  There was a little clam,
    & his given name was Sam. . . .

Nonsense, to be sure, but displaying a certain amount of ingenuity.

[41] MTP, undated typescript.
[42] Paine, Works, VII, 56, believed this was written about 1865, but he was a decade off. (Bills for a bachelor like Mark Twain?) The rough first draft was written January 7, 1874, and on that day sent in a letter to James T. Fields. (See facsimile pp. 14-15 herein.)
[43] The poem is reprinted and examined in Arthur L. Vogelback, "Mark Twain and the Fight for the *Tribune*," *American Literature*, XXVI, 377-380 (November, 1954).
[44] MTP, Notebook #13, p. 29.

Mark Twain's notebooks are sprinkled with his poetic efforts. Some barely got started, such as his effort to turn Leigh Hunt to political satire in "Abou Ben Butler — (may his tribe $\frac{\text{surcease}}{\text{decrease!}}$)."[45] Hardly more successful was his jingle (22 lines) about his friend James R. Osgood:

> Gaily the Osgoo*dar*
> Smoked his cigar. . . ."[46]

Even his verse for children is better than this. In an 1880 story, which he never published, we find:

> There was a little cat,
> And she caught a little rat,
> Which she dutifully rendered to her mother,
> Who said, "Bake him in a pie,
> For his flavor's rather high —
> Or confer him on the poor, if you'd druther."[47]

This was probably for his daughters, as was "Kiditchin" (17 lines) * five years later. This one was about Jean's pet donkey and he worked in a little German, which the girls were studying.[48]

Mark Twain's deep fondness for Negro spirituals and jubilees is too well known to need documentation here. In his Hartford home he would sit at the piano and sing them for his own pleasure in a quavering tenor. And he never tired of hearing them sung. It is interesting, therefore, to note his efforts to compose his own spirituals:

> Swing him wid de gospel wrath
> & yank him into de gospel path[49]

More polished is "Camp Meeting" (8 lines), which begins:

> Ole Satan's a-*comin'*, *don't you run* —
> $\frac{\text{Slap}}{\text{Heave}}$ on de *ar*mor, git yo' gun —
> Keep *on* a *blazin'*, *hear* de rifle crack!
> Aim for his *bos*om, hit him *in* de back![50]

To tabulate all the brief lines of verse which Mark Twain composed in his notebooks would be tedious and to little point. There are at least

[45] MTP, Notebook #15, p. 10. Butler was a controversial Union general and radical Republican politician.

[46] Ibid., 18-19.

[47] *Concerning Cats: Two Tales by Mark Twain,* ed. Frederick Anderson (San Francisco, 1959), 8.

[48] Paine, *Biography,* 822.

[49] MTP, Notebook #16, p. 16. Written about 1881. Before settling on the word "yank," he canceled "boost," "shove," and "highst."

[50] MTP, Notebook #22, p. 8, August, 1887. There is a separate AMS version, slightly revised, in MTP, DV #152 (6), which Paine has dated, for some reason, "1906-7." © Copyright 1966 by the Mark Twain Company.

Those Annual Bills.

Air — Those Evening Bells.
By Mark Twain.

Those annual bills! those annual bills!
How many a song their discordfull warning
thrills thrills fills tells swell
Of "truck" consumed, enjoyed,
forgot
Since New Year last
Since I reviewed received
Since I was floored, strapped,
fell under, skinned, scalped,
flayed by last year's lot!

Those joyous hours are past away
Those hams
Those minions blithe, O where are they?
Once loved, lost, mourned — now
vexing ills
Your ghosts return in annual bills

aground cleaned

And so will be when I am broke;

old yearly duns will still go around

That annual

While bards than I more frantic still

While other bards shall
with frantic quills

Shall damn & damn these
annual bills!

Hartford, Jan. 7/74

My Dear Fields:
I send this original rough draft just as it was when I laid the pen down to welcome you two hours ago. If you had only opened my cheque-book (which lay under the MS.) you would have found New-Year's inspiration there for even a more gifted poem than this one is.

I am glad! to send this to you, since you were complimentary enough to ask it. Yrs ever
Saml. L. Clemens.

J. T. Fields
148 Charles St.
Boston.

three better indications of his concern for things poetic during the 1870's. It was in this decade, most likely, that he began his burlesque play about Hamlet. Of the fragments which are preserved, several are in blank verse.[51] Then there is his popular complaint about the power of a catchy jingle to drive one to distraction. His "Literary Nightmare" swept the nation in 1876, as newspapers and magazines reprinted his history of the "horse-car poem" with its catchy chorus:

> Punch, brother! Punch with care!
> Punch in the presence of the passenjare![52]

The third of these miscellaneous pieces is the *Fireside Conversation in the Time of Queen Elizabeth,* usually called merely *1601.* This famous piece of bawdiness concerns us here, because so much of the frank conversation is couched in a fair iambic meter, which sometimes has the old-time ring of Shakespearean blank verse. *1601* could never have been written by a man who had not steeped himself in the poetry of Elizabeth's day. [53]

In this connection we should remember, too, the fun Mark Twain had with Shakespeare in *Huckleberry Finn,* Chapter 21. Huck was entranced — and who can blame him! — by the Duke's version of Hamlet's soliloquy (25 lines)*:

> To be or not to be; that is the bare bodkin
> That makes calamity of so long life. . . .

Huck committed this to memory, as he also did Emmeline Grangerford's "Ode to Stephen Dowling Botts, Dec'd" (24 lines)* in Chapter 17. In the latter, Mark Twain was once more lampooning the elegies of Mrs. Moore — probably "Little Charlie Hades" and "Little Libbie," says Walter Blair: "It seems unlikely that Clemens could read verse as touching as this without feeling an urge to emulate it."[54] There is a nice touch in the last lines of the poem, whose meter suddenly shatters in order to ring in a couple of clichés.

Mark Twain's other verse of the 1880's is practically unknown. Most of it has never seen print. "Farewell Darling" (32 lines) is incorporated in an amusing, but unpublished, article entitled "The Great Journalist Interviewed." It is a burlesque interview of Joseph "Pultizer" (*sic*), who purchased the New York *World* in 1883. In the course of the interview, Pultizer recites "a kind of dirge" he dashed off the previous week. He

---

[51] *The Twainian,* pp. 4-6 (June, 1943).
[52] Its first appearance was in *The Atlantic Monthly,* XXXVII, 167-169 (February, 1876).
[53] For *1601* and its background see Paine, *Biography,* 580-581, and *Date, 1601: Conversation as It Was by the Social Fireside in the Time of the Tudors,* ed. Franklin J. Meine (Chicago, 1939).
[54] *Mark Twain & Huck Finn* (Berkeley, Calif., 1960), 212-213.

says, "You can make it bid farewell to anything or anybody you want to."[55] It is intentionally a curious, confusing poem.

The following year, 1884, Mark Twain penned a comic elegy called "My Dog Burns" (12 lines)* about his deceased Hartford pet. He closed with the punning couplet

> Like a good author, thou wast a trusty friend
> And thy tail, like his, red to the very end.[56]

Two years later, when a childhood friend of his wife's got married, he wrote her a humorously didactic poem entitled "S'klk! G'lang!" (25 lines)*.[57] Poetry was for special occasions. The following year, reminded of odd British names while working on his *Connecticut Yankee,* he toyed with such rhymes as "harsh clanks — Marjoribanks" and "dumbly — Cholmondeley."[58] Next came a poetic experiment with Irish and French dialect in the narrative of a French schoolteacher in Killaloe. French manners and morals are both satirized in the light, vigorous little verse (25 lines). The teacher ends up with a "fist betune his eyes."[59] Less successful was Mark Twain's effort to build a poem around the absurd misuse of nautical terms. He began boldly with "The anchor watch was set where the lofty lanyards met," but he soon bogged down.[60]

Now that we have traced Mark Twain's own versifying down through the happy Hartford years, it is time to pause in order to examine his appreciation of the poetry written by others. It would be pleasant to record his fondness for Whitman, his recognition of a great kindred spirit; but there is no evidence that the "barbaric yawp" from Camden meant anything to him. In the winter of 1885-86 he reminded himself, "Send $20 to Walt Whitman, poet."[61] His tribute on Whitman's seventieth birthday makes no mention of Whitman's poetic achievements,[62] nor does the unpublished article in which he defends Whitman against the charge of obscenity.[63] What an irony is here in this mutual indifference

[55] MTP, DV #367.
[56] Sent in a letter to H. B. Stephens and printed in *Every Other Saturday,* I, 457-458 (December 20, 1884). Reprinted in *The Twainian,* p. 3 (July-August, 1953).
[57] First printed in *The Twainian,* p. 3 (May-June, 1963).
[58] MTP, Notebook #22 (I), p. 15a.
[59] MTP, Notebook #24, p. 7.
[60] Part of a skit entitled "Statement of Captain Murchison," MTP, DV #332. He had about 16 lines of verse here.
[61] MTP, Notebook #21, p. 31. Apparently he sent only $10 — the amount solicited from each of thirty-six people; see Thomas Donaldson, *Walt Whitman, the Man* (New York, 1896), 174.
[62] *Camden's Compliment to Walt Whitman . . . ,* ed. Horace L. Traubel (Philadelphia, 1889), 64-65.
[63] MTP, DV #36, a seventeen-page AMS.

— and it *was* mutual — of two writers whose goals had so much in common!

It would be a mistake, however, to assume that it was the seriousness of Whitman that repelled Mark Twain. Up until 1892 Mark Twain himself may have written mostly light, humorous verse, but the poems he cherished most were not of this sort at all. The poems which brought tears to his eyes when he read to his young bride at night were doubtless the amorous, sentimental, religious poems she always loved best.[64] In the ardor of his first romance a young man is never quite himself. He will go to great sacrifices to hold the one he loves. Not often and not for long could Mark Twain stand such poetry as this. These poems, however, probably did help to solidify his taste for conventional rhymes and stanzas. Not for many years was he to branch out himself into free verse. Like many others, he was not yet ready for free verse, while Whitman was writing it.

When he went onto the lecture platform, Mark Twain seldom failed to read at least a poem or two. Once he wrote to a newspaper editor for a copy of a poem he recalled reading in his paper many months before. "I hate to make a reading entirely out of my own pathos," he said.[65] During his 1871 lecture tour he sometimes closed his program with a memorial poem written by James Rhoades after the death of Artemus Ward. "This finale was universally approved," we are told. "Read with feeling, as Mark Twain knew how to read verse, the lines won respect, even of critics who complained of everything else in the lecture."[66] From this time until the end of his life Mark Twain invariably kept both serious and comic poems in his repertoire whenever embarking on a lecture tour.

Not only did he read verse on the platform, but also he loved to recite it from memory to his friends. As far as we know, almost none of this poetry which he committed to memory was humorous. It was, instead, philosophic, stately, inspirational, or nostalgic. He took delight in surprising people with it — perhaps in displaying such an unexpected mark of culture in America's great comic.

It is certain that Mark Twain read poetry constantly. His notebooks are sprinkled with poem titles, as well as with short quotations from poems he liked. Occasionally he copied an entire poem like "The Burial of Moses." His books, too, and his personal correspondence carry such

[64] *The Love Letters of Mark Twain,* ed. Dixon Wecter (New York, 1947), 146. Livy's Scrapbooks (MTP) are filled with such poems as "Perfect Through Suffering" and "The Patter of Little Feet." In her Commonplace Book of 1863-71 (MTP, DV #161) she copied dozens of poems, which progress from silly to sentimental to religious in nature.
[65] Typescript in MTP.
[66] Paul Fatout, *Mark Twain on the Lecture Circuit* (Bloomington, Ind., 1960), 160.

frequent references to poetry that the subject can never have been far from his thoughts.

The range of the poetry he cites is broad. It extends from Heinrich Heine to the raftsmen's ballads of the Mississippi. Pre-Elizabethan rogue songs share his pages with modern square-dance lyrics. Popular songs, sea chanties, Negro spirituals, the great and humble poets of his own day — all these found their way into his writings. Nor did he quote this verse in order to make fun of it — only on a few occasions, as with "post-mortem poetry." As a rule, he quoted seriously. In a way it was as if the relatively unschooled Candidate for Gentility — to use Brooks's phrase — were trying hard to come to terms with the purest art form which employed the tools of his own trade, namely, words.

In poetry, as elsewhere, Mark Twain's likes and dislikes were strong. In 1884 he was enraged when some "literary louse" dedicated "his garbage" to Howells.[67] But in 1874 he had sent his friend a poem by "a child of 17," hoping *The Atlantic Monthly* would print it.[68] On several occasions he did all he could to befriend poets who were down on their luck.[69] Time and again he expressed enthusiasm over certain poems he had encountered, usually in the magazines. As late as 1902 he was requesting Howells' support in "discovering" a young Japanese poet whose work he enclosed.[70] Although he knew what he liked, he was not sure it was real poetry. He needed to have his judgment confirmed.[71] When dealing with his wife and not with literary men, his deference vanished and his assurance returned. On such an occasion he demonstrated to her that a certain woman's poem was incomparably superior to Longfellow's poem on the same old legend.[72]

Even to his wife, however, Mark Twain confessed that *no* one could pass good judgment upon all varieties of literary work: "If they were to set *me* to review Mrs. Browning, it would be like asking you to deliver judgment upon the merits of a box of cigars."[73] And he instinctively realized his own limitations as a poet. Early in 1879, for example, he wrote to Howells about an ancient Roman vessel, whose herbs continued to emit a fragrance after 1,500 years. He said he was sending a clipping about the vessel to Thomas Bailey Aldrich, a good friend and poet. He

[67] *Mark Twain–Howells Letters,* ed. Henry Nash Smith and William M. Gibson (Cambridge, Mass., 1960), II, 488.
[68] Ibid., I, 34-35.
[69] Ibid., II, 325-327; *Love Letters,* 171.
[70] *Mark Twain–Howells Letters,* II, 739.
[71] For example, see his letter to Irving S. Underhill on May 30, 1900, Berg Collection, New York Public Library.
[72] MTP, unpublished letter of January 20, 1872.
[73] Clara Clemens, *My Father: Mark Twain* (New York, 1931), 47.

added, "Thought Aldrich could do a sonnet on it."[74] Here, Mark Twain recognized, was a poetic theme, but one too subtle, too fragile for his own pen.

As do most people, Mark Twain considered poetry an adjunct to special occasions. "Aldrich must be about 60," he wrote Howells. "Let's lay for him and celebrate it with some dreadful poems."[75] At banquets and other functions in his own honor, he listened with great pleasure to poems about himself. Sincere and polished tributes were written to him by such poets as Oliver Wendell Holmes and Henry VanDyke. These he adored, quite naturally, but apparently with no greater appreciation than he adored the pretentious tribute mailed to him by a Judge Kirlicks from Texas. He broke a rule and included Kirlicks' poem in his autobiography.[76] (Both *The Century* and *Harper's* had rejected it.) It almost seems as if Mark Twain naively hoped that poetry might help to cloak him with a mantle of respectability, if not even of immortality.

In the case of poetry *not* written either about himself or by his friends, Mark Twain could spot an untrue ear as quickly as false sentiment. In the late 1870's he marked up his copy of *The Poetical Works of Levi Bishop*. He consigned it to his Library of Hogwash. The most enlightening marginal note takes the form of a stanza which Mark Twain offered as a substitute for a stanza of Bishop's "jingling twaddle." What he objected to here seems to be the faulty ear, the lack of music, the commonplace diction, the poor fusing of sound and sense:

> Then strike anew Columbia's anthems!
> The nation's birth-day dawns again;
> On each return, Oh, shout ye millions!
> Let distant ages swell the strain.

In the margin Mark Twain has written his flamboyant stanza:

> Then roll the booming blasting thunder
> Then belch the hateful smoke abroad.
> The heavens shall shout the mighty wonder
> And gates of hell shall cry aloud.

And beside this he scribbled, "*Any*body can write poetry."[77]

Since Mark Twain in this example is too obviously sacrificing meaning for sound, a more significant item is his translation of "Die Lorelei"*. Living abroad in 1878-79, Mark Twain had been studying German and translating nursery rhymes into that language to amuse his children.[78]

---

[74] *Mark Twain–Howells Letters,* I, 250.
[75] Ibid., II, 546.
[76] May 18, 1907, a still unpublished installment in MTP.
[77] MTP. © Copyright 1966 by the Mark Twain Company. This third edition of Bishop's book was printed in Detroit in 1876.
[78] MTP, DV #155, contains several such manuscripts.

Now, to help his new travel book *A Tramp Abroad,* he was reading Rhine legends. It was here that he came across L. W. Garnham's translation of Heine's beautiful poem. He reprinted it with a comment that the measure was "too nobly irregular" and did not "fit the tune snugly enough." He was right. Garnham's translation *is* unsingable, unpoetical. It begins:

> I do not know what it signifies,
>   That I am so sorrowful?
> A fable of old Times so terrifies,
>   Leaves my heart so thoughtful.

Mark Twain was so displeased with this that he made his own translation of the six stanzas. It is incomparably better, wedding itself naturally to the lovely tune:

> I cannot divine what it meaneth,
>   This haunting nameless pain:
> A tale of bygone ages
>   Keeps brooding through my brain:

There can be no doubt that Mark Twain worked hard at this, although he belittled the result: "It may not be a good one, for poetry is out of my line. . . ."[79] Unwarranted modesty was part of his stock in trade, just as was outrageous bragging.

Because so much has been made of Mark Twain's speech at the Whittier Birthday Banquet in Boston in 1877, a word is needed here. Poets are involved. Well known is the desolating silence which is supposed to have greeted his speech. To many it seemed that the speech took in vain the hallowed names of Emerson, Longfellow, and Holmes. Whether or not Mark Twain was evidencing a spirit of rebellion — conscious or unconscious — against the conservative bards of New England is something we may never know. One thing is certain, however, as Henry Nash Smith points out: his use of quotations from twelve different poems "shows a quite respectable familiarity with the texts."[80] As for the aftermath, we should not forget that Mark Twain was invited to the reception and breakfast for Holmes two years later, that Holmes wrote him that charming poem in 1885, and that Mark Twain participated in the Authors' Readings at the Boston Museum in 1887 for the Longfellow Memorial Fund. In other words, as Smith has proved, Mark Twain's "mistake" at the banquet was less "hideous" than we have imagined.

At about the time of this banquet Mark Twain was introduced to Fitzgerald's translation of the *Rubáiyát.* The serene philosophy of Omar

---

[79] *A Tramp Abroad,* Works, IX, 123-126.
[80] " 'That Hideous Mistake of Poor Clemens's,' " *Harvard Library Bulletin,* IX, 172 (Spring, 1955).

Khayyám made him a quick convert. A faithful convert, too. Even late in life he might interrupt a billiard game at any moment to recite:

> For some we loved, the loveliest and best
> That from his vintage rolling time has prest,
> > Have drunk their cup a round or two before,
> And one by one crept silently to rest.
>
> Ah, make the most of what we yet may spend,
> Before we too into the dust descend;
> > Dust unto dust, and under dust to lie,
> Sans wine, sans song, sans singer, and — sans End.[81]

A notebook entry in the summer of 1885 states simply, "Perfect: Abou ben Adhem & the Rubiyat [sic]."[82] More than twenty years later he wrote that "the more a disciple gets of Omar the thirstier he becomes."[83] And in 1906 Mark Twain told his biographer that no poem had given him so much pleasure through the years. "It is the only poem I have ever carried about with me," he said. "It has not been from under my hand all these years."[84]

One senses that Omar's philosophy was hardly more interesting to him than was Fitzgerald's remarkable translation — if, indeed, it can be called a translation. In 1909 Mark Twain complained to his best friend about a graceless new version of the *Rubáiyát:* "Why, Joe, it is as if the organ-monkey should reconstruct the Overture to Tannhäuser & go discording it around town on his hurdy-gurdy happy & unashamed. . . ."[85] And in the early 1890's, when Mark Twain was getting ready to wage his own war against God, he must have found inspiration in Fitzgerald's lines, for he copied many of them into his notebook:

> O Thou! who didst with pitfall & with gin
> Beset the Road I was to wander in,
> Thou wilt not with Predestined Evil round
> Enmesh, & then impute my fall to sin![86]

Time and again Mark Twain was to shape his own verses to this success-ful form.

We come now to Robert Browning. This enthusiasm of the late 1880's may have helped to sober Mark Twain's attitude toward poetry in general. It is surprising that Browning appealed to him so strongly. Their personal acquaintanceship may have helped; also the robust vigor of certain poems. At any rate, he was proud in 1886 to be elected Reader to a Browning

---

[81] Paine, *Biography,* 614-615.
[82] MTP, Notebook #19, p. 25.
[83] MTP, HNS file, ALS to James[?] Logan, February 2, 1907.
[84] Paine, *Biography,* 1295.
[85] MTP, ALS to Joseph Twichell, January 1, 1900.
[86] MTP, Notebook #26, pp. 37-38.

class, which met weekly in the Clemens library. It was delightful work, he said, even though it took him three days to prepare an hour's reading — "And mind you, I'm on the ABC only — his *easy* poems."[87] At first he prepared "a modest small lecture" for each session. One time, at least, a prominent Browning scholar came to give a reading.[88]

So popular were these classes that guests begged to attend. After a year Mark Twain was justly proud of his performance as Reader and of never having lost a member of the class by desertion. Characteristically, he passed it off with a jest: "All you need in this life is ignorance & confidence; then success is sure . . . put me in the right condition & give me room according to my strength, & I can read Browning so Browning himself can understand it."[89] Members of the Browning class long remembered these sympathetic readings, which gave such marvelously clear insight into obscure poems. They did not all realize the effort it cost Mark Twain. Before reading a poem, he studied it word by word, digging out every layer of meaning possible. His elaborate pencil markings in *Men and Women*[90] indicate every shade of emphasis in reading which would help to reveal the poet's purpose. And we can be certain that he did not mar these readings with his Southwestern drawl. Paul Fatout assures us that, when Mark Twain read Browning on the platform in 1895, his drawl disappeared altogether, as "the humorist was completely suppressed by the serious literary man. . . ."[91]

There were evening readings, too, around the library fire. The neighborhood was invited to hear Mark Twain read aloud from many poets. "He liked stirring poetry," recalls his nephew, "which he read admirably, sometimes rousing his little audience to excitement and cheers. Shakespeare remained, by whatever name, the love of his heart. . . ."[92] Incidentally, the first words set in type by Mark Twain's fantastic Paige machine were "William Shakespeare."

How incongruous all this seems in the man who was himself writing verse like "Kiditchin" and "S'klk! G'lang!" up until about 1890. By then his intense study of Browning combined with the increasing sobriety of his outlook to turn his verse into more serious channels. From this time onward almost three-fourths of his poetic composition was serious in nature.

[87] *Mark Twain to Mrs. Fairbanks,* ed. Dixon Wecter (San Marino, Calif., 1949), 258-259.
[88] Professor Corson of Cornell, author of a new book on Browning. Ibid., 260-261.
[89] MTP, typescript of letter to Mrs. Foote from Hartford, December 2, 1887. © Copyright 1966 by the Mark Twain Company.
[90] MTP. See also Paine, *Biography,* 846.
[91] *Mark Twain on the Lecture Circuit,* 246.
[92] Jervis Langdon, *Samuel Langhorne Clemens* (memorial pamphlet published about 1935), 14-15.

His first serious efforts after 1890 seem rather conventional and derivative, sparked by no genuine passion. Perhaps that is one reason it cost him such labor to worry out the four quatrains which begin:

> The Singer holds the flag-watch in the field;
> Beside him rests his dinted war-worn brand;
> And greets with stirring song the tranquil night,
> And singing strikes his harp with bloody hand:
>
> "The lady whom I worship name I not,
> Though long have I her colors loyal borne,
> I gladly fight for Freedom and for Light
> And for the flag whereto my faith is sworn."[93]

This frankly romantic cry of benevolence and patriotism was no small departure for Mark Twain in the field of poetry. As we shall see, events at the turn of the century were to give him second thoughts about swearing faith to one's flag.

Less romantic and more philosophic is the very rough draft of a He-She dialogue which Paine dates "80s or 90s." The optimistic woman believes that "unselfishness" exalts people, bringing them closer to what she terms "The Great Image." The man, disillusioned, does not agree:

> The trait whereof you speak
> I have not seen in him. It is a freak
> Of his too plastic fancy to misclaim
> This non-existent grace.[94]

Rather obviously, this was an early attempt to put into verse the argument he later expanded into *What Is Man?* Polemic poetry of this sort, even though it failed, was another step in the growth of Mark Twain.

During the 1890's two other poets joined Shakespeare, Browning, and Omar Khayyám in his particular esteem. They were Kipling and Shelley, strange bedfellows. Even had he not been captivated personally by Kipling the man, he would have been excited by the dash and originality of his poems. They were at his own level. He read them over and over again, he said, finding them ever animated by truly human, genuine emotions.[95]

Mark Twain's enthusiasm for Kipling seems quite natural. Not so his

[93] MTP, DV #113. This pencil AMS and another, DV #152 (7), show Mark Twain's notes, deletions, and changes while composing. Paine dates it "Probably 80s," but its mood seems post-Browning. Also, the many German words on the six work-sheets indicate that he may have written it while abroad in the 1890's. © Copyright 1966 by the Mark Twain Company.
[94] MTP, DV #332. © Copyright 1966 by the Mark Twain Company.
[95] See especially Paine, *Biography,* 1440, and Elizabeth Wallace, *Mark Twain and the Happy Island* (Chicago, 1913), Chapter 10, "The King Reads Kipling." (Mark Twain was often called "The King" in his later years.) Also, in MTP see the clipping from the *South African Register,* October 14, 1895.

fondness for Shelley. This latter interest was directly stimulated by his reading a biography which tried to whitewash the poet's private life. Mark Twain dipped his pen lightly in hell as he wrote "In Defense of Harriet Shelley" for the *North American Review* in July, 1894. To prove his points, he quoted more than 60 lines of Shelley, often in very brief excerpts. DeLancey Ferguson is convinced that Mark Twain never wrote a more brilliant piece of prose than this "masterpiece of destructive analysis." It is all the more amazing, he adds, because, "Of all the English poets, Shelley, it would seem, was the one whom Mark Twain was least likely to understand. But he did."[96] His interest in Shelley endured, also. After 1900 he read "Ode to a Skylark" to an impressionable audience at the Waldorf.[97] And as late as 1909 he was perusing books about Shelley, as well as rereading favorite poems.[98]

The 1890's were tragic years for Mark Twain. Prior to his world tour of 1895-96 even the very lightest poem which he prepared for publication during this decade had a sickly hue. He called it "Love Song" (26 lines)*. It is a burlesque and he pretended to have submitted it for the prize at the International Medical Convention in London in 1881.[99] The burlesque is more bitter than comic, however, and the poem was probably written in pain at a German health resort in 1891-92.

The gayest poem of the early 1890's was not for publication. It was entered in the guest book of his good friend Laurence Hutton, then literary editor of *Harper's Magazine*. He called it "Last Meeting & Final Parting."

> When I meet you I shall know you,
> By your halo I shall know you —
>   Thus shall know you, blameless man;
> And you'll know me also, Larry,
> When we meet but may not tarry —
>   Yes, alas, alas, you'll know me by my fan.[100]

Above the verse Mark Twain sketched two men, one with a halo, the other with a fan.

---

[96] *Mark Twain: Man and Legend*, 255.
[97] *Mark Twain Himself*, produced by Milton Meltzer (New York, 1960), 223.
[98] Wallace, *Mark Twain and the Happy Island*, 131.
[99] See his note to Howells with the manuscript, MTP, Paine #263. Charles Neider dates the poem 1895 in *Mark Twain: Life as I Find It*, 231, and Merle Johnson gives its first printing as 1896 in *Bibliography*, 128. However, it appeared in the *Medical Fortnightly* (St. Louis), May 15, 1892; see *The Twainian*, p. 6 (April, 1944).
[100] Johnson, *Bibliography*, 136, says that this appeared in *The Critic*, November, 1904. (See facsimile p. 26 herein.) *Talks in a Library with Laurence Hutton*, recorded by Isabel Moore (New York, 1905), facing p. 308, has a photostat of the poem dated by Mark Twain on July 5, 1890. Two other verses to Hutton were in letters of October 30, 1892, and February 5, 1893. Typescripts are in MTP.

The Last Meeting, & Final Parting

When I meet you I shall know you,
By your halo I shall know you —
    Thus shall know you, blameless man;
And you'll know me also, Larry,
When we meet but may not tarry —
    Yes, alas, alas, you'll know me by my fan.

                                        Mark Twain

Onteora, July 5, 1890.

These years also brought forth his most moving love lyric. He entitled it "The Earth Invoketh the Sun" and inscribed it "(To Livy, November 27, 1892)"* — probably for her birthday the next day.[101] It is not the sincerity of the emotion which surprises us, or even the extended imagery. It is rather that Mark Twain should display such skill in prosody. The unusual stanza, the repetition with variation, the smooth flow, the alliteration, the beautiful symmetry of the whole — these, together with the imagery and feeling, make it a new departure for Mark Twain, despite the poetic diction.

To the best of Mark Twain's recollection it was about 1893 that he wrote "The Derelict" (68 lines)*.[102] This is another poem which deserves to be known better. Having pondered the sad fates of Lord Clive and Warren Hastings, Mark Twain was moved to take the imaginary case of an old man in an almshouse, muttering about his former greatness. At the request of his wife and daughter Susy, he wrote it as a poem, sensitive and pathetic. Ten years later the forgotten manuscript turned up. Mark Twain read it aloud to the household in Elmira and seems to have liked it so well that he wrote "Copyright by S. L. Clemens, 1904" at the bottom of the first page.[103] Five years later, a year before his death, he read the poem to Paine, who found it strong and impressive. "I should call it good, I believe," agreed Mark Twain, to whom the poem now seemed almost another man's work. "There is no figure for the human being like the ship," he added, "no such figure for the storm-beaten human drift as the derelict. . . ."[104] "The Derelict" is one of Mark Twain's most lucid and touching poems.

In a lighter vein at about this time Mark Twain translated eleven poems from what he called "the best known book in Germany."[105] This was Dr. Heinrich Hoffmann's *Der Struwwelpeter,* a genuine classic for children. The poems — all rather long — explain the horrible things that happen to children who do such things as play with matches, suck their thumbs, or pull the wings off flies. My own German nurse brought me up on Mark Twain's translation of *Slovenly Peter.* This was more than forty years ago, but the poems and their frightening illustrations are still vivid in my memory. Perhaps *too* vivid!

[101] From a previously unpublished AMS quoted in Caroline T. Harnsberger, *Mark Twain: Family Man* (New York, 1960), 53.
[102] This was a popular title, but none of the other poems which I have located are like Mark Twain's. Even Kipling's in 1894 is quite different.
[103] MTP, DW #10. © Copyright 1966 by the Mark Twain Company. This is the only complete version of the poem I have seen. Johnson, *Bibliography,* 136, is misleading. Langdon, *Samuel Langhorne Clemens,* 22-24, tells of the rediscovery of the poem and prints all but the last verse.
[104] Paine, *Biography,* 1500.
[105] Mark Twain's translation, complete with illustrations and "The Translator's Note" dated Berlin, October, 1891, was published by the Marchbanks Press of New York in 1935 for the Limited Editions Club. A handsome book.

We move now into the latter part of the decade, where we find the well-known "L'Arbre Fée de Bourlemont" (20 lines)*. This gentle song of the children runs like a musical motif throughout the novel *Joan of Arc* (1896). The children of Domremy sing it to the Fairy Tree.[106] Albert E. Stone, Jr., who has made a special study of *Joan of Arc,* believes that the Fairy Tree is "the central symbolic vehicle for Mark Twain's pastorale" and that "The Tree and song together constitute Clemens's most notable addition to the Joan of Arc legend."[107]

These three poems alone of 1892-95 — "The Earth Invoketh the Sun," "The Derelict," and "L'Arbre Fée de Bourlemont" — should help prove that Mark Twain no longer regarded his own poetry primarily as a medium for satire and comedy. Each of these poems is completely earnest in a different way, each reveals a marked skill in prosody, and each is brought to an effective conclusion.

Bleak as these years were, however, the fun had not left Mark Twain completely. Numerous poems after 1895 testify to this. Just before embarking on his world tour, for example, he wrote a dozen lines or so of comic verse which he called "Contract with Mrs. T. K. Beecher"*. (Her husband had helped marry him and Livy.) The little verse is noteworthy for two reasons only: it is written on thin leaves of stone, and in a whimsical way it states his disbelief in any form of afterlife.[108]

In the course of his round-the-world lecture tour in 1895-96 the aging Mark Twain had plenty of time at sea. Once more he used shipboard leisure to make verse. His notebooks contain several ill-fated attempts to compose humorous poems about Australia and India. Since he was following his old practice of including a poem or two in each reading, it is likely that he was trying to work up a fresh, original poem for his repertory — a poem both topical and completely new to his audience. First he made a short try at a verse entitled "Lyric," which was to be a farce about a jackass and a jackass bird.[109] Then he tried to get something started with "The Moa came down like a sheep on the fold." After a dozen futile lines he gave this up, too.[110] Not in his notebook, but surely of this period, is an attempt to weave into verse some of the colorful names of India. The poem begins with "The Rudyard of Kipling, the Rajah of Swat" and moves into such tongue-twisters as

> Jansettjee Curvettjee Manockerjee Ram
> Shapoorjee Jivadjee he cares not a dam

[106] Works, XVII, 13-14.
[107] "Mark Twain's *Joan of Arc:* The Child as Goddess," *American Literature,* XXXI, 15-16 (March, 1959). The original AMS version of the poem is in MTP, DV #145. The novel was serialized anonymously in *Harper's Magazine* in 1895-96.
[108] The poem appears in Paine, *Biography,* 1002, and was first published in *Munsey's Magazine,* October, 1895.
[109] MTP, Notebook #28a (II), p. 63.
[110] Ibid., 63-64.

Later, he was to succeed in completing a poem with Australian names. This first time, however, after some 30 lines he bogged down.[111]

While crossing the Pacific, Mark Twain made initial efforts to prepare a poem about Australian animals. It must have annoyed him that he was unable to ready the poem for the platform until after he had left Australia and was on his way to Ceylon. From then on the poem seems to have been a feature of his performance. Newspapers in India and South Africa singled out what they called the "Australian Poem" (20 lines) for special praise.[112] A triumph as presented on stage by its author, the poem looks flat in cold print. He called it "Invocation"*.[113]

For Chapter 36 of his travel book *Following the Equator,* Mark Twain composed a longer poem which is reminiscent of his stillborn Indian verse. He called it "A Sweltering Day in Australia" (48 lines)*. First he listed eighty-one names of Australian towns, which he said were "good for poetry." Then he crammed sixty-six of these names into a dozen stanzas "To be read soft and low, with the lights turned down."[114] A moment's practice will show that Mark Twain was right, that these *are* good words for poetry. And who is so uncharitable as to balk at the meaning of lines which sound so beautiful?

The long tour, however, was a racking physical strain. Most of Mark Twain's ill-humor found its usual safety valve in his private notebooks. It may have been the imperialistic war in South Africa that turned his thoughts to death, for it was there he began a bitter poem:

> O, Death, thou sceptred king with a reptile's soul!
> Basest of all the tribe of shabby gods
> Commission'd to hunt insulted man.
> O pitiless misuser of dear & noble powers,
> Scoffer at prayers, grantor of none;
> > Answering all with *NO:*
> Sparing the old & weary, pleading for release
> Slaying the young & happy:[115]

This was all he wrote on the subject at the time, not dreaming that his daughter Susy would take ill and die before the end of that very summer.

[111] MTP, Paine #84, contains the rough holograph, together with notes for *Following the Equator* (1897).
[112] MTP contains a number of such clippings from newspapers along his route.
[113] *Mark Twain's Notebook,* 264. Paine has done some editing of the poem as worked up in the original Notebook #28a (I) and #28b in MTP.
[114] Underlinings for reading accent are found in the AMS, which is in MTP, Paine #84. The manuscript has one stanza which Mark Twain canceled and left out of his book.
[115] MTP, Notebook #29 (II), p. 50. The second half of this is very rough and has been canceled. The restoration is mine. © Copyright 1966 by the Mark Twain Company.

It was not long after her death that he jotted in his notebook four lines entitled "Life." They haunt the memory with overtones of meaning:

> We laugh and laugh,
> Then cry and cry —
> Then feebler laugh,
> Then die.[116]

During the next ten years, 1896-1905, Mark Twain wrote a great deal of poetry. Except for two short trifles that need not delay us, and except for the Australian and Indian poems noted above, the poems of this decade were all serious. Feeble fun was to break out again in his verse five years before his death, as if to follow the design of "Life" above. But this final laughter came in brief, sporadic bursts, whereas the serious poems that preceded it were generally more sustained, occasionally quite elaborate.

Perhaps best known of these serious poems is "In Memoriam: Olivia Susan Clemens" (67 lines)*, which appeared in *Harper's Magazine* and is in his collected works.[117] It is the manuscript of this poem which was sold recently in the auction mentioned above (p. 1). At Lake Lucerne on the first anniversary of Susy's death, Mrs. Clemens spent the day re-reading her daughter's old letters, while Mark Twain closed himself in his study to pour out his emotions in verse.

Paine, who was close to the author, considered this a beautiful poem, "lofty, tender, and dirge-like — liquidly musical, though irregular in form."[118] The poem does have beauties, to be sure; but today we are more apt to see it as a "transparently sincere although trite utterance."[119] The triteness may owe in part to the fact that Mark Twain was on unfamiliar ground. Never before in verse had he sought to recollect in tranquility the tender emotions of days gone by. It had been his custom to deride sentiment, to regard most of its manifestations as artificial sentimentalism. Just twenty years before this he had written to a boyhood friend: "As to the past, there is but one good thing about it, & that is that it *is* the past — we don't have to see it again. There is nothing in it worth pickling for present or future use. Each day that is added to the past is but an old boot added to a pile of rubbish — I have no tears for my pile, no respect, no reverence, no pleasure in taking a rag-picker's hook & exploring it. . . ."[120] Yet here he was himself, on the first an-

---

[116] *Mark Twain's Notebook*, 346.
[117] *Harper's Magazine*, LCV, 929-930 (November, 1897). Also in Works, XXII, 384-386.
[118] *Biography*, 1047.
[119] *Mark Twain–Howells Letters*, II, 668.
[120] *Mark Twain's Letters to Will Bowen*, ed. Theodore Hornberger (Austin, Tex., 1941), 23-24. MTP contains the apparently unmailed original AMS.

niversary of a great grief, exploring the past, paying reverence, shedding tears. That he chose to pay reverence in *poetry* speaks eloquently for his respect for the vehicle. And that once again he abandoned set meter and rhyme places him in advance of the popular verse of his own day.

Two more times was Mark Twain to spend a day mourning his daughter in numbers. Except for his broadside of 1871, these elegies were the longest poems he ever wrote. Like the first, each was composed on August 18, the date Susy died. "Broken Idols" (199 lines) was written in Austria in 1898.[121] The other was entitled "In Dim & Fitful Visions They Flit Across the Distances" (230 lines)* and was put together in 1902.[122] The latter is an extensive reworking of "Broken Idols," with a number of passages carried over almost intact. Large sections, however, have been transposed and many new lines added. As in the 1897 elegy, the verse of both poems is free and the meter is roughly iambic.

Perhaps influenced by Browning, the poems take the form of dramatic monologues by a woman who has lost her child. Grief has driven her insane, so that she believes she has lost *four* children. No central image dominates these poems. The woman simply recalls scenes from the past, expressing a love and grief and guilt which are at times embarrassingly intense. Most original and most curious is the sense of guilt — and very Twainian. To the poet who seeks to comfort her she explains how she punished the child on occasion. Then she asks:

> It was not wrong? You do not think me wrong?
> I did it for the best. Indeed I meant it so.
> And it was done in love — not passion; no,
> But only love. You do not think me wrong?
> 'Twould comfort me to think I was not wrong. . . .
> If I had spoken! If I had known — if I had only known![123]

Mark Twain realized that these poems were not great literature. Yet they sprang from a full heart, cost him hours of unaccustomed effort, and he did not wish the final results to perish. So it was that during the dictation for his autobiography on February 2, 1906 (his wedding anniversary), he requested, "Insert somewhere in this chapter my unpublished verses — the insane lady who thought she had lost three children, but it was only one."[124] His memory played him false on the number of children. Two years later he was reminded again of these verses, while dictating a description of his Aquarium. This was a private club of Angel-

[121] Paine, *Biography,* 1177-1178, gives a different origin for the poem, but the AMS is dated by Mark Twain "Aug. 18, 1898, Ischl." MTP, HNS file.
[122] MTP, DV #220. It is from this that Paine quotes 86 lines in *Biography,* Appendix U.
[123] MTP, DV #220. The dots at the end of line 5 are Mark Twain's. © Copyright 1966 by the Mark Twain Company.
[124] MTP, marginal note in original typescript of autobiography.

fish, girls ten to sixteen, whom he had selected as sort of honorary grand-children.[125]

So much for Mark Twain's poetic outpourings about his lost Susy. Apparently his heart was too full to brook confinement to regular meter and rhyme. He generally lacked the patience to carve the cherry pit or polish the gem. "It is harder," he once said, "to make a maxim than to do right." He may have been discovering that it was harder still to make a true poem.

For her birthday in 1898 Mark Twain gave his wife a handsomely illus-trated volume of Stevenson's Scottish poems, folksy and sentimental. But two months later he himself was back at the job of making disenchanted verse in the pattern of his beloved *Rubáiyát*. His first attempt was with the morbid notion — later expanded into prose[126] — that the human body was designed by God primarily as a breeding place for microbes. "The Microbe-God" (12 lines) is in rather rough form, beginning:

> From Cradle unto Grave I keep a house
> Of Entertainment where may drowse
>   And feed & ~~swill~~ dis-ease germs — and
>   in a wild
> Their species procreate & carouse[127]

Dissatisfied, he crossed out his three incomplete stanzas and began anew on the opposite page. This time he entitled the poem "Age — A Ru-báiyát" (16 lines). As before, the more distant he got from Fitzgerald, the more trouble he had. The emphasis this time was on the pathos of old age and the nothingness of all existence:

> And maunder feebly over That & This
>   Thinking we think — we do but dream —
> And wonder why our $\frac{\text{moonings}}{\text{maundrings}}$ go amiss[128]

Ten years later Mark Twain returned to his microbe theory, suggesting that the most valuable cargo on the Ark was really the microbes in the bodies of Noah's family. The "heaven" or favorite resort of the microbes was the great intestine, which they lauded in their principal hymn:

> Constipation, O constipation,
>   The joyful sound proclaim
> Till man's remotest entrail
>   Shall praise its Maker's name.[129]

[125] Ibid., April 17, 1908. It was at this time that he misled Paine about the genesis of "Broken Idols."
[126] MTP, DV #348-349, entitled *3,000 Years Among the Microbes* (361-page AMS). Shorter unpublished manuscripts on this theme are DV #12 and DV#13.
[127] MTP, Notebook #32, p. 46a. © Copyright 1966 by the Mark Twain Company.
[128] Ibid., 47. © Copyright 1966 by the Mark Twain Company.
[129] *Letters from the Earth,* ed. Bernard DeVoto (New York, 1962), 31.

While residing at a Swedish health resort late in 1899, Mark Twain wrote an amusing sketch, "My Boyhood Dreams."[130] He showed how some of his old friends like Howells, Aldrich, and Cable had failed to achieve their dreams of becoming ringmasters, barkeeps, and horse doctors. He then composed a long and very unamusing poem "To the Above Old People" (80 lines)*. He lifted a few lines from "The Microbe-God," since he was using again the *Rubáiyát* stanza and repeating his disillusioned theme. One stanza will suffice to convey his un-Browninglike attitude toward the last of life:

> For every nickled Joy, marred and brief,
> We pay some day its Weight in golden Grief
>   Mined from our Hearts. Ah, murmur not —
> From this one-sided Bargain dream of no Relief!

The poem ends with a welcome to Death as a relief from the sufferings of old age.

Six years later Mark Twain pursued this theme in another long poem entitled "Apostrophe to Death" (48 lines)*. Although it has never seen print, the condition of the existing manuscripts and typescripts suggests that he may have had publication in mind.[131] The first part of the poem is an attack on the Calvinist God, predestination, and original sin. Why, for example, should the blameless child "fry in hell for Adam's sin?" After these early polemics, the poem raises a sort of Whitmanian hymn to Death:

> O Death, the only kind & dear & generous!
> Sole of all the gods of all the heavens
> That does not keep a trader's shop & peddle benefits;
> Whose unbought mercy is for all alike; whose pity & whose peace
> Go free to all, unsmirched by bargain-taint;
> Whose gentle refuge standeth wide
> To all that weary are: the soiled, the pure,
> The rich, the poor, the unloved & the loved!

The poem was written in Dublin, New Hampshire, during the idle summer holidays of 1905, just a year after the death of his wife. He did not mourn her in poetry as he had his daughter. Her death was more expected — a relief from long illness. With the passing of friends and loved ones, however, Mark Twain's loneliness increased. The face of Death no longer angered or frightened him.

Personal bereavements and God and death were not the only things to awaken Mark Twain's Muse during these troubled years. The world

[130] First published in *McClure's Magazine,* January, 1900. Also in Works, XXIII, 259-261.
[131] MTP, Paine #122, contains a rough AMS draft, a fairly clean AMS copy, plus two different typescripts. © Copyright 1966 by the Mark Twain Company.

was misbehaving in specific ways which caused him to seek an outlet in secret verse. In 1898 he began a scathing attack on a cowardly assassin of his day with the line "His soul is made of politics. . . ."[132] The 16 lines, however, are too rough to quote effectively.

The following year he reacted violently to a Kipling poem and dashed off a harshly worded reply — secret, of course. Kipling's new poem "The Absent-Minded Beggar" extolled patriotic Britons for volunteering to fight the Boers. Mark Twain had been in South Africa recently and his natural sympathy was with the outmanned Boers. His own stanza, therefore — also entitled "Absent-Minded Beggar" — would have shocked his English friends and neighbors:

> Duke's son, earl's son, son of the noovo rich,
> Bilk's son, snob's son, bastard son of a bitch,
> > None of 'm whine, they *all* jine,
> > Jine the cavalree,
> And hell they raise for God his praise
> In the Boer his counteree.
> > Pay, pay, goddam you, pay.[133]

Meanwhile, global conditions were forcing Mark Twain to think about imperialism. When the Spanish-American War brought his own nation into what he called the European Game, he was most unhappy:

> Rally round the flag, boys, rally once again
> Shouting the battle cry of Boodle — treason.
>
> Columbia the sham of the Ocean
> Up with the traitor & down with the[134]

He could not seem to get started. Then suddenly he found another patriotic song for his satire. He called his poem "The Battle Hymn of the Republic (Brought down to date)" (20 lines)*. It opens: "Mine eyes have seen the orgy of the launching of the Sword. . . ." Although a tongue-twister to sing, the poem is regular in its meter and fearless in its assault on Manifest Destiny.[135]

The most interesting poem written by Mark Twain on this hot issue of imperialism is "My Last Thought" (82 lines)*.[136] He left his manuscript of this poem in the pages of a Filipino novel which contained a shorter

---

[132] MTP, Notebook #32 (II), pp. 42-43.
[133] MTP, DV #152 (1), pencil AMS. I ignore two changes he made in the second line. © Copyright 1966 by the Mark Twain Company.
[134] MTP, DV #74. With the word "treason" the MS changes from ink to pencil, suggesting a later attempt. © Copyright 1966 by the Mark Twain Company.
[135] MTP, DV #74, a neat ink AMS. Printed very inaccurately in Philip S. Foner, *Mark Twain: Social Critic* (New York, 1958), 278.
[136] MTP, Paine #6, a clean, neat AMS with only four slight revisions in its nine pages. © Copyright 1966 by the Mark Twain Company.

poem of the same title. This shorter poem is supposed to have been written by a Filipino patriot just before execution. It prays for peace, happiness, and freedom in his native land. Mark Twain, whose heart was with the natives, couched his most cogent criticisms of imperial conquest in the monologue of a dying President of the United States. Belatedly the President is ridden by guilt. He entreats his supposedly moral and outraged countrymen (what irony Mark Twain must have seen in this!) to remember his erstwhile good deeds and to forgive his later crimes. "I meant my country well," he pleads,

> I erred through weakness, not intent. For I
> Was overborne by sordid counsels,
> Base ambitions, & from my head I took
> The precious laurel I had earned, & in its place
> I set this poor tin glory, now my wear,
> Of World-Power, Conqueror of helpless tribes,
> Extinguisher of struggling liberties!

The dimming eyes of the President take passing comfort in seeing the glorious old Flag once more. Then his vision clears for a horrible moment and he cries:

> The stars are gone, a Skull & Bones
> Are in their place; the Red Bars are there,
> But soaked with guiltless blood;
> The White Bars are Black —
> Hide it from my sight.

"My Last Thought" is not a satire on McKinley or Roosevelt or anyone in particular. It voices the guilt of a nation and, more specifically, the guilt of Mark Twain himself. When the Spanish-American War had begun, he was living in Austria. Reports of the war caused him at first to glorify it as the noblest war in history. Later he saw his mistake. When America "snatched the Philippines," he felt that she stained the flag. Whereas his revised "Battle Hymn of the Republic" was a slashing, bitter indictment of imperialism, "My Last Thought" expressed in tones of pathos the humanitarian's grief over tyrannies committed around the world in the name of Christendom. Both poems are effective and both are among Mark Twain's few anti-imperialist writings of any merit which our government and publishers are accused of conspiring to suppress.

After his long elegies on Susy and after these poems about old age, death, and world conquest, Mark Twain was done forever with turning meter to serious use. In the twilight of his days, back he went to the short light verse of his youth. Of the eighteen poems I can attribute to this period, 1906-10, only one is longer than eight lines and only one is serious.

The longer poem (16 lines) is a bawdy bit written for a meeting of the Mammoth Cod Club.[137] The serious one is a political invective. Its mood and language are like those of his "Absent-Minded Beggar." Mark Twain's diminishing confidence in the democratic electorate also shows in these lines:

> Ho, burghers of Dutch Albany!
> Ho, buggers of New York!
> Ho, sons of bitches from the slums
> And painted whores from Cork!
> Ho, pimps & bilks from Hell's Delight!
> Ho, convicts, prison-nursed
> Oh, rally, rally, to the polls,
> And 'lect the bloody Hurst![138]

This piece stands out in violent contrast to his other poems of the period. These others are for humor alone. Not one of them is worth quoting here. Twice he composed risqué stanzas after the *Rubáiyát*[139] and again in his notebook he jotted a men's-club verse.[140] Two poems deal with his pet game of billiards, several are nonsense rhymes, and five were dashed off for and about specific friends, usually his Angel-fish. He was in his seventies now, content to sit by the fireside and read poetry, not write it.

Some of what he read he consigned to the literature of "hogwash." In attacking Mary Baker Eddy, he took special pains to deride her poetry, which was pretentious but childlike.[141] On the other hand, he encouraged and befriended young Witter Bynner, when he quit his job in order to write poetry.[142] With joy he devoured the breezy Western poems of Eugene P. Ware, old "Ironquill."[143] And on a train in 1909 he came across Willa Cather's "Palatine" in the newspaper and remarked to Paine, "Here is a fine poem, a great poem, I think. I can stand that."[144]

Imperialism notwithstanding, the poems of Kipling continued to thrill Mark Twain, as did the *Rubáiyát*. His love for Holmes's "Last Leaf"

---

[137] MTP, privately printed copy in HNS file.
[138] Ignoring two small deletions, I quote from MTP, Notebook #38, p. 19. This is a more finished version of the working manuscript in the Berg Collection, New York Public Library. MTP, DW #20, is a typescript of the latter and bears a note that "Hurst" might be W. R. Hearst, who aspired to the New York governorship in 1906. © Copyright 1966 by the Mark Twain Company.
[139] MTP, DW #23.
[140] MTP, Notebook #38, p. 18. Possibly he picked this up somewhere. Unless there are signs of editing, it is sometimes hard to identify these short verses, which appear in his notebooks without comments, credits, or quotation marks.
[141] See especially *Christian Science*, Works, XXV, 80-81.
[142] See letter of October 5, 1906, addressed "Dear Poet," typescript in MTP.
[143] Paine, *Biography*, 1374.
[144] Ibid., 1501.

never diminished. It was one of those scraps of verse, he said, which take hold of us and stay in our memories: "It is like a dreamy strain of moving music, with no sharp notes in it."[145] Gray's "Elegy" was another favorite. He was fond of quoting from it in these last years and one of his Angel-fish was persuaded to memorize it during her visit with him in 1907. She was urged, however, to learn a shorter poem next time, for "there is something about a long poem," he said, "that acts as a narcotic, no matter how good it is."[146]

Despite this comment, his admiration for Shakespeare remained firm. Only the year before his death he became so excited about the Bacon-Shakespeare controversy that he wrote *Is Shakespeare Dead?* It seemed impossible to him that the man who wrote the jingle on the Stratford grave could be the same man who produced the poems and plays. No one, he warned, who has read the noble verses of the plays should follow them by reading "Good friend for Iesus sake forbear." "It will give him a shock. You never notice how commonplace and unpoetic gravel is until you bite into a layer of it in a pie."[147]

This book about Shakespeare would not have entered the mind of a man who hated poetry. The truth is that in his old age Mark Twain was drawn more and more to an appreciation of poetry. Poems about himself he was still frank to glory in: "I love poetry — at least I love it when it advertises me."[148] One poetic tribute he found so moving when he heard it that he could not trust his voice to reply.[149] Poetry was also an increasing source of comfort to his melancholy spirit. Sitting on a verandah in New Hampshire in 1906, he said he was "broken hearted, in a Garden of Eden. . . . I felt as Alexander Selkirk felt, who had to cheer himself with sorrowful poetry. . . ."[150]

At home for small gatherings he continued his old practice of reading selections from the great poets. He seems never to have wearied of this. How lonesome he must have been in 1909 and 1910 in his vast new mansion of Stormfield after his daughter Clara had married and his daughter Jean had died. Then he was truly alone. For solace at the time of Jean's burial, he turned to poetry, as other people may turn to prayer. He read aloud lines he remembered from his mourning for Susy thirteen years before:

[145] Works, XXVI, 232, from his *Harper's* article on Howells. See also Paine, *Biography*, 1555-56.
[146] Dorothy Quick, *Enchantment* (Norman, Okla., 1961), 90-91.
[147] Works, XXVI, 362-363.
[148] MTP, unpublished autobiography, September 13, 1907. See also December 28, 1906.
[149] Rough draft of letter, 1907, in MTP.
[150] MTP, unpublished autobiography, June 11, 1906.

When last came sorrow, around barn and byre
  Wind-carven snow, the year's white sepulchre lay.
"Come in," I said, "and warm you by the fire":
  And there she sits and never goes away.[151]

Our survey is finished. More poems by Mark Twain will come to light
in the future, but it is unlikely that they will change the present picture.
We have already seen that Mark Twain's interest in poetry was far more
extensive than has been imagined. In his own compositions he moved
from trite love poems to parodies and satires and humor, then into verse
of deadly seriousness, and finally back to comedy. We recall his prophecy:

  We laugh and laugh,
  Then cry and cry —
  Then feebler laugh,
  Then die.

To compare Mark Twain's early verse to his late is a bit like comparing
a clown to a tragedian. In their unpretentious areas, many of the early
poems are quite successful. The serious poems are less spontaneous, but
their lack of gusto is offset by the increase in emotional and intellectual
content. They show also that Mark Twain had improved in poetic imagi-
nation, sensitivity, and discipline. His good ear and his originality were
qualities he had from the start; but it took time for him to cultivate
expository power, verbal felicity, and — above all — a genuine respect for
poetry as a vehicle of serious expression.

Once he had cultivated this respect in the 1890's, there was scarcely a
major theme of his prose which did not find voice in his poetry. He
mourned lost loved ones, he quarreled with God, and he bared his sense
of personal guilt. He gave sympathy to fallen grandeur and he argued
that no human motive can be unselfish. He scouted the voting public, he
alternately cursed and hailed Death, he glamorized the importance of the
microbe, and he inveighed against imperial conquest, both Europe's and
America's.

To collect even the published poetry of Mark Twain into one volume
is to expose its incredible disparity. The worst is embarrassing. The best
may not make the soul soar, but it is good enough and extensive enough
to prove that here is a novelist who did more than merely dabble in verse.
The range of his poetry in both topic and mood is immense. The triviali-
ties and "hogwash" are offset by poems of unquestionable power in a
number of diverse fields.

These better poems form a solid core of competent, sometimes impres-

[151] Paine, *Biography,* 1551.

sive, work. They help suggest that Mark Twain's so-called "literary declaration" about detesting poetry has been common currency far too long. No man who truly hates poetry is going to write so much of it. Nor will such a man spend countless hours of his lifetime in reading, studying, criticizing, memorizing, and reciting poems. Such a man will simply leave poetry alone, so long as it is harmless. It may take time for us to learn to ignore Mark Twain's hasty declaration and to convince ourselves that the evidence all proves that, in truth, he *loved* poetry.

Note on the Texts &

Most of the poems which follow are based on the available texts of the first printed editions. I have taken only such slight liberties as correcting upside-down letters, supplying obvious periods and forgotten quotation marks, and correcting several obvious typographical errors. Spelling has been left as it was. Dialect verse like "Three Aces" and "A Ballotd" has been proofread letter by letter.

Those poems and stanzas printed here for the first time follow the original manuscripts in the Mark Twain Papers. They are published by consent of and are © copyrighted in 1966 by the Mark Twain Company. In most cases I have not cluttered the page by indicating Mark Twain's cancellations.

All of these poems are printed in their entirety. Appearances to the contrary, there are no ellipses. Mark Twain was generally a good speller but a creative punctuator, often using series of dots or asterisks.

THE HEART'S LAMENT

To Bettie W——e, of Tennessee

I know thou wilt forget me,
For that fond soul of thine
Turns boldly from the passionate,
And ardent love of mine.
It may be, that thou deemest it
A light and simple thing,
To strike with bold and nervous arm,
The heart's lone mystic string.

Thou wilt not deign to hear the strain,
Thy own dear hand hath woke;
It matters not if ne'er to thee
It's [*sic*] troubling echoes broke.
I know — ay, well, thou wilt forget
I ever dreamed of thee;
Thou lovest not, thou carest not,
My fettered soul to free.

Tho' gay and gifted crowd thee around
The beautiful are thine —
Then how canst thou, oh, lofty one,
Kneel at a lonely shrine?
I ask it not; oh, never more
My soul's cry shalt thou hear —
My heart shall learn in bitterness,
To hide its love so dear.

Rambler.

Hannibal *Daily Journal,* May 5, 1853.
Reprinted in C. J. Armstrong, "Mark
Twain's Early Writings Discovered,"
Missouri Historical Review, XXIV, 493
(July, 1930).

LOVE CONCEALED

To Miss Katie of H——l

Oh, thou wilt never know how fond a love
    This heart could have felt for thee;
Or ever dream how love and friendship strove,
    Through long, long hours for mastery;
How passion often urged, but pride restrained,
    Or how thy coldness grieved, but kindness pained.

How hours have soothed the feelings, then that were
    The torture of my lonely life —
But ever yet will often fall a tear,
    O'er wildest hopes and thoughts then rife;
Where'er recalled by passing word or tone,
    Fond memory mirrors all those visions flown.

For much I fear he has won thy heart,
    And thou art but a friend to me;
I feel that in thy love I have no part,
    I know how much he worships thee!
Yet still often will there rise a gleam of hope,
    Wherewith but only time and pride can cope.

RAMBLER

Hannibal *Daily Journal,* May 4, 1853. Reprinted in Minnie M. Brashear, *Mark Twain, Son of Missouri* (Chapel
Hill, N.C., 1934), 121.

Married in Podunk on the 3rd ultimo, by the Rev. D. Willis,
Mr. H. Hoe with Miss Anne Handle, all of that city.

How useless an Handle without any Hoe,
    And useless a Hoe without any Handle;
No better a winter without any snow,
    Or a candlestick minus a candle.

But here, joined in one, the Handle and Hoe
    With life's rugged journey, smooth over,
And each prove a helper in this world below,
    Till death shall hoe both to another.

Hannibal *Daily Journal,* May 7, 1853. Reprinted
in Brashear, *Mark Twain,* 146.

[GOOD-BY, GOOD-BY]

Good-by, good-by,
I bid you now, my friend;
And though 'tis hard to say the word,
To destiny I bend.

Just before leaving Hannibal at the end
of May, 1853, Mark Twain wrote this
in the autograph album of Ann Virginia
Ruffner, one of his girl friends. See
Julian L. Street, *Abroad at Home* (New
York, 1920), 252.

THE BURIAL OF SIR ABNER GILSTRAP,
EDITOR OF THE BLOOMINGTON *REPUBLICAN*.

Parody on "The Burial of Sir John Moore."

Not a drum was heard, nor a funeral note,
    As his corpse to the ramparts we hurried;
Not a soldier discharged his farewell shot,
    O'er the grave where our hero we buried.
            — Burial of Sir John Moore.

Not a sound was heard, nor a funeral note,
    As his carcass through town we hurried;
Not e'en an obituary we wrote,
    In respect for the rascal we buried.

We buried him darkly, at dead of night —
    The dirt with our pitchforks turning;
By the moonbeams' grim and ghastly light,
    And our candles dimly burning.

No useless coffin confined his breast,
    Nor in sheet nor in shirt we bound him;
But he lay like an Editor taking his rest,
    With a Hannibal Journal round him.

Few and *very* short were the *prayers* we said,
    And we felt not a pang of sorrow;
But we mused, as we gazed on the wretch now defunct —
    Oh! where will he be tomorrow?

The "Iron Horse" will snort o'er his head,
    And the notes of its whistle upbraid him;
But nothing he'll care if they let him sleep on,
    In the grave where his nonsense hath laid him.

Slowly, but gladly we laid him down,
    From the field of his fame fresh and gory;
We carved not a line, we raised not a stone,
    To mark where we buried a tory.

Hannibal *Daily Journal*, May 23, 1853. Reprinted in Brashear,
Mark Twain, 138-139.

[TWO STANZAS FOR HIS MOTHER]

Carson City, Jan. 30, '62.

My Dear Mother:

"How sleep the brave who sink to rest,
    Far, far from the battle-fields's dreadful array,
With cheerful ease and succulent repast,
    Nor ask the sun to lend his streaming ray."

Bully, isn't it? I mean the poetry, madam, of course. Doesn't it make you feel just a little "stuck up" to think that your son is a — Bard? . . . Never mind the *sense* — sense, madam, has but little to do with poetry. [He then goes on to explain how he "patches" together lines from other poems.]

Keokuk *Gate City*, March 6, 1862.

Carson City, March 20, 1862

My Dear Mother:

Lo! the poor Indian, whose untutored mind,
Impels him, in order to raise the wind,
To double the pot and go it blind,
    Until he's busted, you know.

I wrote the three last lines of that poem, Ma, and Daniel Webster wrote the other one — which was really very good for Daniel, considering that he wasn't a natural poet.

Keokuk *Gate City*, June 25, 1862. For both these poems see Edgar M. Branch, *The Literary Apprenticeship of Mark Twain* (Urbana, Ill., 1950), 230-233.

THE AGED PILOT MAN

On the Erie Canal, it was,
    All on a summer's day,
I sailed forth with my parents
    Far away to Albany.

From out the clouds at noon that day
    There came a dreadful storm,
That piled the billows high about,
    And filled us with alarm.

A man came rushing from a house,
    Saying, "Snub up your boat I pray,
Snub up your boat, snub up, alas,
    Snub up while yet you may."

Our captain cast one glance astern,
    Then forward glancèd he,
And said, "My wife and little ones
    I never more shall see."

Said Dollinger the pilot man,
    In noble words, but few, —
"Fear not, but lean on Dollinger,
    And he will fetch you through."

The boat drove on, the frightened mules
    Tore through the rain and wind,
And bravely still, in danger's post,
    The whip-boy strode behind.

"Come 'board, come 'board," the captain cried,
    "Nor tempt so wild a storm;"
But still the raging mules advanced,
    And still the boy strode on.

Then said the captain to us all,
    "Alas, 'tis plain to me,
The greater danger is not there,
    But here upon the sea.

So let us strive, while life remains,
    To save all souls on board,
And then if die at last we must,
    Let. . . . I *cannot* speak the word!"

Said Dollinger the pilot man,
    Tow'ring above the crew,
"Fear not, but trust in Dollinger,
    And he will fetch you through."

"Low bridge! low bridge!" all heads went down,
    The laboring bark sped on;
A mill we passed, we passed a church,
    Hamlets, and fields of corn;
And all the world came out to see,
    And chased along the shore
Crying, "Alas, alas, the sheeted rain,
    The wind, the tempest's roar!
Alas, the gallant ship and crew,
    Can *nothing* help them more?"

And from our deck sad eyes looked out
    Across the stormy scene:
The tossing wake of billows aft,
    The bending forests green,
The chickens sheltered under carts
    In lee of barn the cows,
The skurrying swine with straw in mouth,
    The wild spray from our bows!

            "She balances!
            She wavers!
Now let her go about!
    If she misses stays and broaches to,
We're all" — [then with a shout,]
            "Huray! huray!
            Avast! belay!
            Take in more sail!
            Lord, what a gale!
Ho, boy, haul taut on the hind mule's tail!"

"Ho! lighten ship! ho! man the pump!
    Ho, hostler, heave the lead![1]

And count ye all, both great and small,
    As numbered with the dead!
For mariner for forty year,
    On Erie, boy and man,
I never yet saw such a storm,
    Or one 't with it began!"

So overboard a keg of nails
    And anvils three we threw,
Likewise four bales of gunny-sacks,
    Two hundred pounds of glue,
Two sacks of corn, four ditto wheat,
    A box of books, a cow,
A violin, Lord Byron's works,
    A rip-saw and a sow.

A curve! a curve! the dangers grow!
    "Labbord! — stabbord! — s-t-e-a-d-y! — so! —
Hard-a-port, Dol! — hellum-a-lee!
    Haw the head mule! — the aft one gee!
Luff! — bring her to the wind!"

"A quarter three! — 'tis shoaling fast!
    Three feet large! — t-h-r-e-e feet! —
Three feet scant!" I cried in fright
    "Oh, is there *no* retreat?"
Said Dollinger, the pilot man,
    As on the vessel flew,
"Fear not, but trust in Dollinger,
    And he will fetch you through."

A panic struck the bravest hearts,
    The boldest cheek turned pale;
For plain to all, this shoaling said
A leak had burst the ditch's bed!
And, straight as bolt from crossbow sped,
Our ship swept on, with shoaling lead,
    Before the fearful gale!

[1] Due to a printing error the next 19 lines appear on p. 374 instead of p. 373 of the first edition of *Roughing It* — Ed.

"Sever the tow-line! Cripple the mules!"
    Too late! . . . . . There comes a shock!
        * * * * * *
Another length, and the fated craft
    Would have swum in the saving lock!

Then gathered together the shipwrecked crew
    And took one last embrace,
While sorrowful tears from despairing eyes
    Ran down each hopeless face;
And some did think of their little ones
    Whom they never more might see,
And others of waiting wives at home,
    And mothers that grieved would be.

But of all the children of misery there
    On that poor sinking frame,
But one spake words of hope and faith,
    And I worshipped as they came:
Said Dollinger the pilot man, —
    (O brave heart, strong and true!) —
"Fear not, but trust in Dollinger,
    For he will fetch you through."

Lo! scarce the words have passed his lips
    The dauntless prophet say'th,
When every soul about him seeth
    A wonder crown his faith!

For straight a farmer brought a plank, —
    (Mysteriously inspired) —
And laying it unto the ship,
    In silent awe retired.

Then every sufferer stood amazed
    That pilot man before;
A moment stood. Then wondering turned,
    And speechless walked ashore.

Roughing It (Hartford, 1872), 369-375. Written 1864.

A RICH EPIGRAM [two versions]

Tom Maguire,	Tom Maguire,
Roused to ire,	Torn with ire,
Lighted on McDougal;	Lighted on McDougall;
Tore his coat,	Grabbed his throat,
Clutched his throat,	Tore his coat,
And split him in the bugle.	And split him in the bugle.
For shame! oh, fie!	Shame! Oh, fie!
Maguire, why	Maguire, why
Will you thus skyugle?	*Will* you thus skyugle?
Why curse and swear,	Why bang and claw,
And rip and tear	And gouge and chaw
The innocent McDougal?	The unprepared McDougall.
Of bones bereft,	Of bones bereft,
Almost, you've left	See how you've left,
Vestvali, gentle Jew gal;	Vestvali, gentle Jew gal —
And now you've smashed	And now you've slashed,
And almost hashed	And almost hashed,
The form of poor McDougal.	The form of poor McDougall.

San Francisco letter to the Virginia City *Territorial Enterprise,* December, 1865.
The version at the left appears in Paine's *Biography,* 275-276. The other is from
a newspaper clipping in Mark Twain's Scrapbook, Yale University Library.

NURSERY RHYME

Come, now, Macdougall!
      Say —
      Can lucre pay
For thy dismembered coat —
Thy strangulated throat —
Thy busted bugle?

Speak thou! poor W.J.!
      And say —
      I pray —
If gold can soothe your woes,
Or mend your tattered clothes,
Or heal your battered nose,
Oh bunged-up lump of clay!

      No! — arise
      Be wise!
Macdougall, d——n your eyes!
Don't legal quips devise
To mend your reputation,
And efface the degradation
      Of a blow that's struck in ire!

But 'ware the execration,
Unless you take your station
In a strategic location,
In mood of desperation,
And "lam" like all creation
      This infernal Tom Maguire!

Virginia City *Territorial Enterprise,*
December 20, 1865. In spite of the
spelling, Macdougall is the victim in
the previous piece. Clipping in Mark
Twain's Scrapbook.

HE DONE HIS LEVEL BEST

Was he a mining on the flat —
    He done it with a zest;
Was he a leading of the choir —
    He done his level best.

If he'd a reg'lar task to do,
    He never took no rest;
Or if 'twas off-and-on — the same —
    He done his level best.

If he was preachin' on his beat,
    He'd tramp from east to west,
And north to south — in cold and heat
    He done his level best.

He'd yank a sinner outen (Hades),*
    And land him with the blest;
Then snatch a prayer 'n waltz in again,
    And do his level best.

He'd cuss and sing and howl and pray,
    And dance and drink and jest,
And lie and steal — all one to him —
    He done his level best.

Whate'er this man was sot to do,
    He done it with a zest;
No matter *what* his contract was,
    HE'D DO HIS LEVEL BEST.

* Here I have taken a slight liberty with the original MS. "Hades" does not make such good metre as the other word of one syllable, but it sounds better. [Mark Twain's note. Supposedly the verse was written by Simon Wheeler, narrator of the Jumping Frog tale.]

The Celebrated Jumping Frog of Cala-veras County, and Other Sketches (New York, 1867), 37-38.

THE MYSTERIOUS CHINAMAN

Once upon a morning dreary, while I pondered, weak and weary,
Over many a quaint and curious shirt that me and Steve has wore,*
While I was stretching, yawning, gaping, suddenly there came a tapping,
As of some one gently rapping, rapping at my chamber door —
"I guess it's Maim," I muttered, "tapping at the chamber door —
    At least — it's she, if nothing more."

Presently my soul grew stronger — hesitating then no longer,
"Maim," said I, "or Fannie, truly your forgiveness I implore;
But the fact is, I was washing, and so gently you came sloshing,
And so faintly you came sloshing, sloshing round my chamber door,
That I scarce was sure I heard you" — here I opened wide the door —
    Ah Chang was there — and nothing more!

Then this leathery wretch beguiling my sad fancy into smiling,
By the grave and stern decorum of the countenance he wore —
"Though thy crest be shorn and shaven, thou," I said, "art sure no Raven,
Ghastly, grim and long-tailed scullion, wand'ring from the kitchen floor —
Tell me what thy lordly will is, ere you leave my chamber door."
    Quoth Ah Chang, "No shabby '*door.*'" (*hic!*)

Much I marveled this ungainly brute to hear discourse so plainly,
Though his answer little meaning, little relevancy bore;
For we cannot help agreeing that no living human being
Ever yet was blest with seeing Chinaman outside his door
    With message like "No shabby 'door.'"

* The sacrifice of grammar to rhyme, in the second line, is a "poetic license"
which was imperatively demanded by the exigences of the case. — M. T.

First printed in *The Twainian,* p. 3 (July-August, 1947), but written about
1864-65 for the album of "M. E. G.," perhaps a young relative of his San Francisco roommate Steve Gillis of line 2 in the poem.

THE BURIAL OF SIR JOHN MOORE

And other parties, subsequently to the Destruction of the Sennacherib.

The Assyrian came down like a wolf on the fold,
    The turf with our bayonets turning,
And his cohorts were gleaming in purple and gold,
    And our lanterns dimly burning.

And the tents were all silent, the banners alone,
    When the clock told the hour for retiring —
The lances unlifted, the trumpet unblown,
    Though the foe were sullenly firing.

And the might of the Gentile, unsmote by the sword,
    As his corse to the ramparts we hurried,
Hath melted like snow in the glance of the Lord,
    O'er the grave where our hero we buried.

For the Angel of Death spread his wings on the blast,
    And smoothed down his lonely pillow,
And breathed in the face of the foe as he passed —
    And we far away on the billow!

And the eyes of the sleepers waxed deadly and chill,
    As we bitterly thought on the morrow,
And their hearts but once heaved and forever grew still,
    But we spake not a word of sorrow!

And there lay the steed, with his nostril all wide,
    In the grave where a Briton hath laid him
And the widows of Ashur are loud in their wail,
    And o'er his cold ashes upbraid him.

And there lay the rider, distorted and pale,
    From the field of his fame fresh and gory,
With the dew on his brow and the rust on his mail —
    So we left him alone in his glory!

In Mark Twain's twenty-fourth letter to the Sacramento *Union*, June, 1866. Reprinted in Walter F. Frear, *Mark Twain and Hawaii* (Chicago, 1947), 411-412. Mark Twain enjoyed making composite poems.

MY RANCH

I have a ranch of quite unknown extent,
    Its turnips great, its oats without compare;
And all the ranches other men may rent
    And [*sic*] not like mine — so not a dern* I care

'Tis all my own — no turnstile power may rise
    To keep me outward from its rich domain;
It hath a fence that time itself defies,
    And all invaders must climb out again.

'Tis true sometimes with stones 'tis overcast,
    And troublous clods offend the sens'tive sight;
Yet from the furrows I these so quickly blast,
    Their radiant seams do show more clear and bright.

It hath a sow — *my* sow — whose love for grain
    No swearing subject will dispute;
Her swill is mine, and all my slops her gain,
    And when she squeaks my heart with love is mute.

MARK TWAIN

* This imprecation is a favorite one out in the ranching districts, and is generally used in the society of ladies, where only mild forms of expression may be indulged in. [Mark Twain's note.]

The Californian, October 28, 1865. Reprinted in *Sketches of the Sixties by Bret Harte and Mark Twain,* ed. John Howell (San Francisco, 1926), 188-190.

POLONIUS' ADVICE TO HIS SON—
PARAPHRASED FROM HAMLET

Beware of the spoken word! Be wise;
    Bury thy thoughts in thy breast;
Nor let thoughts that are unnatural
    Be ever in acts expressed.

Be thou courteous and kindly toward all —
    Be familiar and vulgar with none;
But the friends thou hast proved in thy need,
    Hold thou fast till life's mission is done!

Shake not thy faith by confiding
    In every new-begot friend,
Beware thou of quarrels — but, in them,
    Fight them out to the bitter end.

Give thine ear unto all that would seek it,
    But to few thy voice impart.
Receive and consider all censure,
    But thy judgment seal in thy heart.

Let thy habit be ever as costly
    As thy purse is able to span;
Never gaudy, but rich — for the raiment
    Full often proclaimeth the man.

Neither borrow nor lend — oft a loan
    Both loseth itself and a friend,
And to borrow relaxeth the thrift
    Whereby husbandry gaineth its end.

But lo! above all set this law:
    UNTO THYSELF BE THOU TRUE!
Then never toward any canst thou
    The deed of a false heart do.

In Mark Twain's eleventh letter to the Sacramento *Union*, July, 1866. Reprinted in Frear,
Mark Twain and Hawaii, 367-368.

MISS SLIMMENS

Air — Auld Lang Syne.

1

Miss Slimmens she's as trim a lass
As any you can find —
She always wears an old brown dress,
All busted out behind.

2

She talketh scandal all day long,
With false malicious tongue —
She'd blast the brightest character
That ever poet sung.

3

She said our ladies, one & all
Were partisans of Jeff
And when they brought her to the scratch
She proved it — o'er the left.

4

On Truman she was monstrous hard,
And hard she was on Brown,
Said they'd a way of nipping cash
Peculiarly their own.

5

She gave Mark Twain an awful shot,
And Kingdom did she lift.
From White & Thayer the fur did fly
Lord! how she snuffed out Smith!

6

She crowded Lewis till he swore
If she would stop the war,
He'd take the cussed newspaper
She corresponded for.

7

She said 'twas funny Baker's charms
No woman could withstand,
But if she saw where those charms lay
She wished she might be cussed destroyed.

8

Now dear Miss Slimmens take a hint,
From this rude song we've sung
And do belay your gossiping,
Trice up your blasted tongue!

To be sung for ushering in New Year's Day, 1867,
aboard ship. Stanza 2 is printed in *Mark Twain's Notebook,* 44. Stanzas 5, 6, and 7 can be found in *Mark
Twain's Travels with Mr. Brown,* ed. Franklin Walker
and G. Ezra Dane (New York, 1940), 63-64. The other
four stanzas are printed here for the first time, © copyright 1966 by the Mark Twain Company.

[IN SORROW I SORROW]

In sorrow I sorrow, O sorrowful day!
In grief-stricken tears O joy speed away!
I weep and I wail, and I waft broken sighs,
And I cry in my anguish, O Woman arise!

But I shout it in vain! for Demons have come,
Who drown my appeal with foul blasphemous tongue;
Yes, in sorrow I fade, and flicker and die!
Lo! a martyr to Suffrage in the tomb let me lie!

St. Louis *Missouri Democrat,* March 12-13, 1867. This
was supposedly written by a woman who signed herself "Secretary of the Society for the Dissemination of
Poetry among the Pawnees" — a woman who said she
was devastated by Mark Twain's attack on female suffrage. Reprinted in *Mark Twain: Life as I Find It,*
ed. Charles Neider (Garden City, N.Y., 1961), 14.

THE MINER'S LAMENT

High on a rough and dismal crag,
 Where Kean might spout, "Ay, there's the rub,"
Where oft, no doubt, some midnight hag
 Had danced a jig with Beelzebub,
There stood beneath the pale moonlight
 A miner grim with visage long,
Who vexed the drowsy ear of night
 With dreadful rhyme and dismal song.

He sang: "I have no harp or lute
 To sound the stern decrees of fate;
I once possessed a two-holed flute,
 But that I sold to raise a stake.
Then wake thy strains, my wild tin-pan,
 Affright the crickets from their lairs,
Make wood and mountain ring again,
 And terrify the grizzly bears.

"My heart is on a distant shore,
 My gentle love is far away,
She dreams not that my clothes are tore!
 And all besmeared with dirty clay;
She little knows how much of late,
 Amid these dark and dismal scenes,
I've struggled with an adverse fate,
 And lived, ah me! on pork and beans.

"Oh! that a bean would never grow,
 To fling its shadow o'er my heart;
My tears of grief are hard to flow,
 But food like this must make them start,
The good old times have passed away,
 And all things now are strange and new;
All save my shirts and trousers gray,
 Three stockings and one cowhide shoe!

"Oh, give me back the days of yore,
 And all those bright though fading scenes
Connected with that happy shore
 Where turkeys grew, and calms and greens —
Those days that sank long weeks ago
 Deep in the solemn grave of time,
And left no trace that man may know
 Save trousers all patched up behind!
And boots all worn, and shoes all torn,
 Or botched with most outrageous stitches.
Oh, give me back those days of yore,
 And take these weather beaten breeches!"

Unidentified newspaper clipping under Mark Twain's name, undated. In possession of Mark Twain Memorial, Hartford.

GOOD BYE

Their voyage done, the fleet that plowed
 Together o'er the main
Spread their broad sails and sped away,
 No more to meet again.

And one shall dance o'er tropic seas
 And under splendid skies
And float like a dream through purple haze
 And the sunset's golden dyes,

Or swim in a glory of amber light,
 Under the mellow moon
And drink the odors that steal on the night
 From the zone of eternal June!

And anchored at last by the beautiful isles
 That garland those tranquil seas,
Shall fold her white wings and fall asleep
 In the hush of an endless peace.

And one shall go forth in the pride of her strength,
　　With the northern blast to play,
Where the storm bird shrieks o'er the billowy waste
　　In a driving mist of spray,

And the spume-flakes fly from the plunging prow
　　Far down on the whistling wind,
And blend their snows with the foamy wake
　　That follows far behind!

And the sullen gloom of the brooding sky
　　Hangs low its awful pall
And darkness the tossing world beneath
　　Where the winking foam-crests crawl!

The thunder peals and the good ship reels
　　Under the tempest's swell,
And the lightning glares on the murky night
　　Like the fateful fires of hell!

Ah, woe to the ship and woe to the crew!
　　(Watcher, pour thy tears like rain!)
For they shall go down in the storm and the night,
　　And be seen no more of men!

Lo, other ships of that parted fleet
　　Shall suffer this fate or that:
One shall be wrecked, another shall sink,
　　Or ground on treacherous flat.

Some shall be famed in many lands
　　As good ships, fast and fair,
And some shall strangely disappear,
　　Men know not when or where.

As the years roll on, the parted may catch
　　Glimpses of former mates
Fading away on Ocean's verge
　　Where night on the gloaming waits:
But never, ah never, while Time shall last
Shall they greet again on Ocean's waste
　　Or by the friendly shore,

The goodly fleet that endured so long
In sisterly concord, calm and storm
    Is parted forevermore!
You cannot but read my riddle aright —
    'Tis well!
Let one pass strangely out of sight,
His mate go down in storm and night:
Sail YOU in tropic seas of light —
    Farewell!

             MARK TWAIN, 1867

At end of *Quaker City* voyage, November, 1867.
First printed in the Cleveland *Plain Dealer,* April
27, 1910. Reprinted in *The Twainian,* pp. 1-2
(June, 1945).

YE EQUINOCTIAL STORM

At three bells of the middle watch,
    When all pure souls did sleep,
A brawling gang round 49
    Their revels wild did keep.

They sang and talked and stories told,
    And lied and laughed and roared,
And woke to fright the neighbors all
    That peaceful lay and snored.

They punches drank and brandy straight,
    And cocktails forty-three,
And set their lungs afloat in floods
    Of tangle-foot whiskee.

Now, Middleton ringleader was
    Of this disgraceful mob,
And Bleydenburg abetted his
    Vile peace-disturbing job.

The "Rajah" and young Dickinson,
    And Captain Queen also,
Did help in this unholy work,
    (The others I don't know).

But Captain Cox and Dr. Shorb,
    And virtuous Marcus Twain,
And Lake and Field did remonstrate
    And begged them to refrain.

It never did a bit of good —
    The villains said " 'twas warm,"
They made no noise, they said, it was
    The equinoctial storm.

The equinoctial storm be blowed!
    No cloud was in the sky.
Let these outlaws be court-martialed
    For this outrageous falsehood.

Aboard ship, 1868. To be sung to the
tune of "Auld Lang Syne." First printed
in the San Francisco *Wasp* in 1884. Reprinted in *The Twainian,* p. 4 (July-
August, 1946).

TROPIC CHIDINGS

SHE

Don't let the sun scan me,
Don't let the wind tan me;
Oh, why don't you fan me?
    It's awfully warm.

Hast thou no feeling
To see the sun peeling,
My cheeks revealing
    Where paint has been?

HE

Thee have I fanned nearly
To death, but you merely
Abuse me sincerely
    And still perspire.

Hast thou no reason,
At such a season,
To look for a breeze on
    A paltry fan?

SHE

Mark, let us sever
Our love forever!
Thus we'll endeavor
    A "coolness" to make.

HE

By George, I'm ready!
By George, I'm willing!
By George, I'm anxious!
    Though it don't rhyme.

Aboard ship, 1868. First
printed in the San Francisco
Wasp in 1884. Reprinted in
The Twainian, p. 4 (July-August, 1946).

ROCK HIM TO SLEEP

Backward, speed backward, Oh! Ball, in your flight!
Make not an ass of yourself — (just for to-night;)
Pull the few silver threads out of your hair,
Fill up and varnish those furrows of care —
Care that was born of attempting Fame's steep,
Which *you* couldn't climb, Ball, whom none rocked to sleep.

O, Bally, come back from the echoing shore!
Cease for a season the public to bore
With your infamous rhymes and your stupid complaint,
For *you* know you are claiming to be that which you ain't.
Oh, drivel no more! — don't snuffle, don't weep —
Hang up your lyre, Ball — *I'll* rock you to sleep.

Now I give you this chance, and I'll give you no more:
For if ever again you offer to pour
From your stale, oozy fount of ineffable bosh
Any more rhyming arguments, Ball, that won't wash,
I'll say to those Westerners, "Rise! Of vengeance drink deep!
Rock him to sleep, boys, rock him to sleep."

A New Jersey harness maker named Ball was claiming authorship of the popular "Rock Me to Sleep, Mother." This appeared in the Cincinnati *Evening Chronicle,* March 4, 1868. Reprinted in *The Twainian,* pp. 2-3 (February, 1943).

THE STORY OF A GALLANT DEED

[Roughly after the meter of *Hiawatha*]

THIS INDENTURE, made the tenth
    Day of November, in the year
Of our Lord one thousand eight
    Hundred six-and-fifty,

Between JOANNA S. E. GRAY
    And PHILIP GRAY, her husband,
Of Salem City in the State
    Of Texas, of the first part,

And O. B. Johnson, of the town
    Of Austin, ditto, WITNESSETH:
That said party of the first part,
    For and in consideration

Of the sum of Twenty Thousand
    Dollars, lawful money of
The U. S. of Americay,
    To them in hand now paid by said

Party of the second part,
    The due receipt whereof is here —
By confessed and acknowledg-ed,
    Have Granted, Bargained, Sold, Remised,

Released and Aliened and Conveyed,
    Confirmed, and by these presents do
Grant and Bargain, Sell, Remise,
    Alien, Release, Convey, and Con-

Firm unto the said aforesaid
    Party of the second part,
And to his heirs and assigns
    Forever and ever, ALL

That certain piece or parcel of
    LAND situate in the city of
Dunkirk, county of Chautauqua,
    And likewise furthermore in York State,

Bounded and described, to wit,
    As follows, herein, namely:
BEGINNING at the distance of
    A hundred two-and-forty feet,

North-half-east, north-east-by-north,
    East-north-east and northerly
Of the northerly line of Mulligan street,
    On the westerly line of Brannigan street,

And running thence due northerly
    On Brannigan street 200 feet,
Thence at right angles westerly,
    North-west-by-west-and-west-half-west,

West-and-by-north, north-west-by-west,
    About ———

    I kind of dodged and the boot-jack [supposedly hurled by his father]
broke the looking-glass.

Part of a prose piece entitled "A Memory," in *The Galaxy*, X, 287 (August,
1870).

TO THE VELOCIPEED

No wonder that yoor day was breef,
No wonder that yoo cum to greef;
This is the pint that seems "a joker,"
That men of sense and not in licker
Shood make sich a bluster and adoo
About a waggin split in 2.

Buffalo *Express,* July 29, 1869. Mark
Twain (probably) pretended to be indig-
nant over his landlady's attack on the vel-
ocipede. He says that she wrote this.

SOROSIS

The shades of night were falling fast,
As through an eastern city passed
A blooming maid in bloomers dressed,
With this device upon her crest,
    Sorosis

Her brows were kind; beneath her vail [*sic*]
Her eyes blazed like a comet's tail,
And like a martial bugle rung
The tones of that outlandish tongue,
    Sorosis!

In happy homes she saw the light,
Where hopes and love made all things bright;
Without the night was drear and black,
And from her lips escaped the shriek —
    Sorosis

"Try not the polls! O maid beware
The scheming politician's snare."
'Twas all in vain the old man cried,
For still that ringing voice replied,
    Sorosis!

"O stay," the young man said, "and rest
Thy waterfall upon this vest!"
A tear stole down her painted cheek,
But still she answered with a squeak,
    Sorosis!

"Beware the baleful company
Of Francis Train and Susan B!"
This was old Greeley's warning knell.
A voice replied, you go to — well,
    Sorosis!

At break of day, as through the street,
The watchman walked his lonely beat,
With heavy eyes and sleepy yawn,
A voice cried through the purple dawn,
    Sorosis!

Next evening, on a rostrum high,
The maiden stood with blazing eye,
While from her lips, serene, but pale,
A voice came, like a northeast gale,
    Sorosis!

                    Somefellow

Buffalo *Express,* August 14, 1869. Probably
by **Mark Twain.**

[CALIFORNIA'S DULL]

California's dull,
For she's lost her Moguls,
    And don't know where for to find them;
But let them alone
And they'll waggle home,
    And carry their tails behind them.

On hearing that two "distinguished China-
men" were returning to California, Buffalo
Express, August 19, 1869. Probably by Mark
Twain.

From "Home and Mrs. Byron"
[Supposedly written by Lord Byron to his aged sister]

O, dearly, I love you my sister Aurusta,
So soft and so gentle, not sullin and crusty;
'Twixt us here shall e'er be constant and true an
Affection like that between Hades and Juan;
That the words shall look off from the page of my glory,
To the *Atlantic Monthly* for that other story.

Buffalo *Express,* September 11, 1869. Probably by Mark
Twain, whose friend and neighbor-to-be, Harriet Beecher
Stowe, had an article in the *Atlantic* about the current Byron
scandal.

[THE LAST WORD]

Mr. Twain:

    Honored Sir — We have seen, from your pen,
An article headed, "Last Words of Great Men."
O, thank you, sir! Bless you! You've started a doubt;
That shall grow till it puts our maligners to rout;
For these great men were married, or some of them were,
That's certain; and we, sir, shall beg to infer,
Hence, the probable end of a charge we have heard,
That a man with a wife never has the last word.
               Yours truly,
                  Some of the Little Women

In Personal column of Buffalo *Express,* September 25, 1869.
Probably by Mark Twain.

THE REASON WHY

"Why don't the men propose, mamma,
    Why don't the men propose?
Each one seems coming to the point,
    And then away he goes."
"They are frightened at your cost, my dear;
    They are thinking of your clothes."

In Gleanings column of Buffalo *Express,* October
4, 1869. Probably by Mark Twain.

[SAYS GOSSIP ONE TO GOSSIP TWO]

Says Gossip One to Gossip Two,
    "While shopping in the town,
Old Mrs. Pry to me remarked,
    Smith bought his goods of Brown."

Says Gossip Two to Gossip Three,
    Who cast her eyelids down:
"I've heard it said to-day, my friend,
    Smith got his goods from Brown!"

Says Gossip Three to Gossip Four,
    With something of a frown:
"I've heard strange news — what do you think,
    Smith took his goods from Brown!"

Says Gossip Four to Gossip Five,
    Who passed [boasted?] it round the town:
"I've heard to-day such shocking news —
    Smith *stole* his goods from Brown!"

Buffalo *Express,* November 2, 1869. Probably by
Mark Twain.

From an article entitled "The Entertainment Yesterday"
in the POLICE COURT column

[Squire Vanderpool, the judge]
John Deming, you convicted stand
    Of beating one John Greiner.
I am in doubt if it be best
    To place on you a fine, or
Commit you to Dick Dalton's charge
    And let you this time try a
Trip to Charley Fellen's place
    Via the Black Maria.

[Peter Eberhardt, grinning at the judge]
Your Honor, though I'd scorn so mean
An act as thrashing this Jim Green;
Yet let me say, most gracious Squire,
To be tried here I've no desire —
No[w] take my bail, and I'll report,
For Justice, at some higher court.

[Lunch-time solo by policeman charged with living on
same street with man who once voted Republican Ticket]
I feel, I feel, I feel, I feel like a played out "star,"
I feel, I feel, I feel, I feel like a played out "star,"
    Ham Best, don't bodder me!
    Ham Best, don't bodder me!

[Patrick Horan, convicted of stealing $3.10]
I am a noble foreigner
    From Limerick in Spain
And, as you please, I'd like to be
    At l[i]berty again.
I'm king bee wid the dimmy crats,
    So pray be on your guard,
Or else next fall you'll find the deuce
    To pay in the Eighth Ward.

[Squire Vanderpool's reply]
Sure Patrick, you varmint,
    I think you have seen
Already this morning
    Too much of "bensine"
Your head's in a muddle,
    Yer snout's all ablaze,
Be away wid ye now
    For a full sixty days.

[Summary of last indictment]
Mr. Henry T. Smith
    Is a rascally cheat
Who wickedly sought
    His poor landlord to beat.
It is painful, indeed,
    The sad story to tell
How he swindled the landlord
    Of Bonney's Hotel.
He ran up a big bill
    Though in finances vested [busted?]
Left his trunk full of bricks
    And got up and dusted.

Buffalo *Express,* probably Wednesday, March 31, 1870, although this page is headed "Tuesday, March 21, 1870" and other pages of the same day's paper bear different dates. Perhaps an April Fool's Day joke? The article and verse are likely by Mark Twain.

[TWO SATIRES ON NAPOLEON III]

NAPOLEON AFTER HAGENAU

Nap is sick and has sent for his doctor, post haste —
 Rhine water and air are just not to his taste,
And the Prussians have taught the intriguing old chap
 That *Sauer kraut's* horribly bad for a Nap!

CHASSEPOT VS. NEEDLE GUN

 There was a little man and he had a little gun, —
'Twas a Chassepot gun, I hear, —
 He went to flearbruck and didn't get a duck,
But he got a little flea in his ear!

 For t'other little man he had a *needle gun,*
With which to defend the border;
 He went to flearbruck and proceeded to cook
The Chassepot goose in short order!

Signed "Hi Slocum" in Buffalo *Express,* August
12, 1870. Probably by Mark Twain.

OLD TIME AND I
By Mark Lemon

Old Time and I the other night
 Had a carouse together;
The wine was golden, warm and bright, —
 Aye! just like Summer weather.
Quoth I, "Here's Christmas come again,
 And I no farthing richer,"
Time answered "Ah the old, old strain! —
 I prithee pass the pitcher."

"Why measure all your good in gold?
    No rope of sand is weaker;
'Tis hard to get, 'tis hard to hold —
    Come, lad, fill up your beaker."
"Hast thou not found true friends more true
    And loving ones more loving?"
I could but say, "A few, a few,
    So keep the liquor moving."

"Hast thou not seen the prosp'rous knave
    Come down a precious thumper?
His cheats disclosed?" "I have, I have!"
    "Well, surely that's a bumper!"
"Nay, hold awhile, I've seen the just
    Find all their hopes grow dimmer."
"They will hope on, and strive and trust,
    And conquer!" "That's a brimmer."

"Tis not because to-day is dark,
    No brighter days before 'em;
There's rest for every storm-tossed bark."
    "So be it! Pass the j[o]rum!"
"Yet I must own I should not mind
    To be a little richer."
"Labor and wait, and you may find —"
    "Halloo! an empty pitcher."

Buffalo *Express,* August 15, 1870. Probably
by Mark Twain.

[MY NAME IT WAS "OLD CHRIS"]

My name it was "Old Chris"
      When I sailed!
I'd a better time than this
      When I sailed!
For I was a fearless rover,
And crossed the ocean over,
A new world to discover,
      When I sailed!

Then I grew old and hoary,
      As I sailed!
Faded was my glory,
      When I sailed!
And a cruel King of Spain
Rewarded all my toil and pain
With a jolly iron chain,
      When I sailed!

Then I thought this rather rough,
      When I sailed!
But my treatment here's more tough,
      Than when I sailed
For I pass both day and night,
Nailed up so close and tight;
None of me's had a sight,
      Since I sailed!

Who would have this believed,
  When I sailed!
And at "Colon" was received,
  Where I sailed!
Say, do you think it just,
That I fall a prey to rust?
I've been mad enough to "bust,"
  Since I sailed!

Signed "Ab O'Riginee" in Buffalo *Express*, September 27, 1870. Probably by Mark Twain. Supposedly this monologue is spoken by the bust of Columbus within a crate. An American Indian is listening.

PERSONAL

A typo stood with stick in hand
  And copy on his case,
But ne'er a type his fingers sought
  For on his classic face
A look of deepest import dwelt,
  As he that copy read —
'Twas in a little graceful fist,
  And this is what it said:

"A nice yung femail gurl with eyes
  "Of deepest likwid blew,
"And amply flowing awburn locks
  "Wich natu-rally grew,
"Wood like aquaintice sweet to maik
  "With vews to matri-mony —
"Adress, post-pade, box forty-six,
  "To Mary jane Mahoney."

He dropped the stick, procured a sub,
   And then straightway indited
An answer to that "personal."
   Next morn he was delighted
A letter to receive — not paid —
   In terms of warmest greeting,
Appointing for that very night
   The place of their first meeting.

He changed his linen, washed his face,
   Put on some borrowed clothes,
And with serene and joyous mien,
   And blushing roman nose,
He sought the gushing Mary Jane —
   That maid with Auburn hair, —
At their appointed rendezvous,
   And found her waiting there.

At once she cried "O typo sweet,
   "My own true love art thou
"Forever till death do us part —
   I'd like ten dollars now.
But scarcely had she grasped the stamps
   When to the swain's dismay
One Smith, who keeps a keno shop,
   Stepped up and thus did say:

"My *wife* and I, young printer man,
   "Must pray you to excuse
"Our further company to-night,
   "Accept our kind adieux."
That typo sadly turned away,
   No smiles now lit his face;
He murmured "sold," then heaved a sigh
   And went back to his case.

Buffalo *Express*, October 28, 1870. Probably
by Mark Twain.

THREE ACES
JIM TODD'S EPISODE IN SOCIAL EUCHRE

I don't go much on little games of keerds played with a stranger,
Sence — durned galoot! — I took a hand on board the Natchez Ranger,
With three smooth chaps that said they'd like to pass the time away
In a little *social* euchre, or some such harmless play.

I never hed sech luck afore, in any spot or place
My hand was frequent *lousy* with both bowers and the ace.
The chap next to me said, "If we was playin this fur lucre
You'd bust us sure! We're lucky that it's only *social* euchre!"

Bime bye the chap on tother side, sez he "If this was poker
And I could diskeerd two keerds, I'd have a little joker;
I'd back my three remainin keerds fur all I could afford,
Agin three keerds in any hand there is around this board!"

I looked mine over. Rich? You bet! I gin a chuckle merry,
And know'd I had him! "Cap," sez I, "you air my huckleberry!"
Then each of us diskeerded two, I had *all aces* back,
And know'd them would lay over any *three* keerds in the pack!

Soft thing? I guess not! "Cap," sez I, "jest name it if you please!"
Sez he, "Wal, sence you air so kind, I'll chip a V on these!"
"Jes so," sez I, "I see your V and go two X's better!"
"That's jest my fix," sez he, "I'm bound that I wont be your debtor."

To cut it short I went fur him, fast as a little wagon,
I had a sure thing — just the hand to make a hot old "brag" on.
My pond got dry. He "called" me. I spread them aces out
And reached fur that thar "pot," I guess, without a lingerin doubt.

"Hold on!" sez he, "them air not good." Sez I, "they can't be beat
By no *three* keerds. Them aces *must* be jest as good as wheat!"
"Wal here's three clubs — a flush." sez he, "a flush will still beat threes,
And capture your three aces and the 'pot' with perfect ease!"

Plucked? Now you're talkin'! I *was* plucked as bare as any goose!
I would hev fit, but I soon seed it wouldn't be no use;
Them three smooth chaps was on it, and wasn't skeered at danger.
Sence then I don't go much on *social* euchre with a stranger!

CARL BYNG

Buffalo *Express,* December 3, 1870. Probably by Mark Twain.

[I NEVER PLAYED AT "VINGT ET UN"]

I never played at "vingt et un,"
But I was sure to "bust,"
I never got into a fight,
Where I didn't get the wust,
I never bought at auction,
When my purchase wasn't a sham,
In fact, I'm an unlucky cuss,
If I ain't may [I] be — , etc. . . .

"Ab. O'Rig Inee" tells of his bad luck,
Buffalo *Express,* December 13, 1870.
Probably by Mark Twain.

A BALLOTD.

OWED PHOR THE TYMZ; not the knusepaper.

By TWARK MAIN, Skulemarster.

Az meditatin bi miselph,
    I thort a phew reflexyuns,
I'm phree to sa, 'twas awl abowt,
    The Kunnettykut elexyuns.
Not noing mutch of Polleightix
    I am in no perzishun
Tu stait the fax in lurned stile,
    For want of eddecashun.

It seams thare wuz an Inglish mon,
    For Govennur did run
Aga'nst wun Jewill, so I hurd,
    An that's the wa't begunn.
This Inglish, he phelt shure to win,
    Koz hee woz backt bi Twead
Hoo woz toe kum from Tamm'nee,
    In this hiz tyme of knead.

A telleighgramme disclosed the plann,
    An hee got skard, I kenn;
At enneigh rayt, Twead di'nt kumm,
    And di'nt shipp hiz menn.
Thenn tha a scckret cawkuss helld,
    Whenn awl, with wun ackord,
Advized the kandydait tu tri
    Hiz oan, awft-tryde Forth Waurde.

The Forth kood bare wun skweezin moar,
    The Fifth still hadd its shair,
An in New Haven polli-*tricks*,
    Hadd awl it well kood bair.
Twas sed that tu thoze sitteigh waurdz,
    So menneigh hadd ben brawt,
The Stait woz revolushuneyzd,
    And nary trick woz kawt.

This yeer tha mustard in their voates,
    Withowt Tweade's votin men;
In cownting, tha just stufft the bocks,
    With ballods, tenn tymes tenn.
So skruperluss did tha abstane
    From kollonizin ruitz,
Thease onnist saants phelt justyphide,
    In making yuse or *stuffz*

"Beetz awl how Inglish runnz," tha sa,
    And then, annon, thare whisst!
Till sum Republykan sudgjests;
    Let'ze look at the chekk Lisst."
When low, wun hunderd ballotz mower,
    Inn tu the bocks hedd gott,
Thann awl hoo voated at the pole —
    Tha pheard that tha woz kawt!

Wun cide most frawd-u-lunt-leigh hadd gande
    Republykans kried, "hoo?"
But Demokrats kept mumm, the while,
    And sed not even, "boo."
Awltho the ballod-bocks woz klosed,
    The luserz was'nt blufft;
Thair moderator sed at wunce:
    "The Stait bocks haz ben stufft."

And hiz Repoart amendid thus,
    Orphishailleigh woz maid,
To the Hi Bored or Kanva-sirs
    And woz befoar them lade.
Then Enfeeld, faimd for riphles, hadd
    Annuther little mattur,
Whitch maid theze dowteigh DemoKrats,
    Riled wuss nor enneigh hattur.

And Chessyear, noated for its cheeze,
    Shee wanted to be hurd
Konsuring twenteigh voats or mower,
    That war throne overbored.
The publick pott woz bilen hott,
    The dorg starr rulde the hower,
Perlit' kulleigh, ov korce, we meen,
    The Hi Bored helld the power;

Then suctch an inkubashun O!
    Sutch *dam*-ming — up the river,
A little Pond was swelled so big,
    Can midwiphe e'er deliver!
Regected woz the voaters prair,
    Konsind to the waist baskitt
Great Lowgan, tho a parteigh cheef,
    And ankshus; durst not ask it.

The thurd Hi Kanvasier, krize owt;
    (Hiz name waz loryer Wallow,)
"Sum notis ov that prair is due,
    Lest Konsekwensez foller."
But eggspectashun's running hi,
    To no hoo wuz elegtid;
Tha maid it owt that Inglish woz,
    Just az thair frends eggspected.

And thenn the Ledgislature sitts,
    To solv the misstory,
And to "eggsamin" furst repoarts —
    Cum deth or vicktory!
Then holeigh horrow seezed the brests,
    Ov Inglish's parteigh friendz;
And thenn begann a hu an kri,
    To gane unlorphul endz.

Tho awl is rong, tha shout: "all rite,"
 "Its constitushunnall,
"That frawd's too sakred to be tuchd,
 Now ceece this greate Karbal."
"The Millertareigh, with Mack chord,
 "Shall jine the prominaiders;
"The sherriffs with thair valyant ades —
 "The *pursy komma taters!*

"And that Hi Hoss will Inglish ride,
 "His Kurridge Kannot phade,
"Hiz plume shal kno whight pheather sho,
 "From out hiz black KoKaid.
"So stand aside yew're but a mob,
 "Ye Ledgislativ krowd!
"If you oppoze, we'll kum to bloze,
 "Great Inglish hee haz voud.

"The Hoss Gardz hee haz knoatyphide
 "The bluddy Sassphields tu,
"The Phoot Gardz now, to Inglish bow,
 "And Nashunals, True Blue.
"The Putnam Falank's ordered owt
 "With soreds hunge bye thair side,
"The Hillyear and the Sitty gards,
 "Their charge — hoo kan abide?

"If blud is shed, enuff's ben sed,
 "We've warned you awl in seeson,
"Hooever's slane, *we're* not to blame,
 "It shurely stands to reeson."
Low! the eventful da apais
 Approaches: and there stood
Brave Inglish, sun of Mars, for war,
 And garments rolled in blud!

Why! Caesar, Wellington; or Grant,
    Such valler didn't no, sur,
McClellan Fallstaff, Butler, pale,
    Bumbastees Phury O' so.
And when that awphul mawn arrives,
    The Ledgislachur meats,
With Juellers and Inglish braves
    In thair respective seets,

They even durst to organize,
    Tho trembling in thair shuze.
And wun poor kuss woz hurd to sa,
    "Are this another *ruze?*"
And soon Kommitteigh men are razed,
    From eather parteigh's rollz,
To see if frawdz or blundering
    Woz practiest at the poles.

Thenn demokrats the war kri raze
    And evreigh throate distends,
Tha pheering lest their kurridge shood,
    Ooze owt thair phinger's endds.
Bold Eaton's men wer tested thenn,
    When hee baid them "dekline,"
Twoz dun, you sea; "Resine," sed hee,
    And so tha awl resine.

Lowd thundurs role, and ranes, tha faul,
    Till rane is turned tu drizzle;
Thair biggest tauke is but a mauk,
    In othur wurds a phizzle.
The wrest ov the Kommittcigh men,
    Go fourth the while to lurn,
Ov Chessyear and the Enfeeld votes;
    The assemblee — tha agjurn.

The Committeihmen, imparshally,
    The boxes over hawl,
And pashuntleigh exhammin lists,
    And make a noat of awl.
Thenn to New Haven sitty strate,
    Tha go, with wun ackord,
In anser to petisheruers
    From grately phamed Forth Ward.

Suffice it, that tha fownd th' excess
    Of Inglish ballods thare;
But just wun hunderd stolen from,
    His rivals skanteigh shair.
Republikans and demokrats
    In holeigh horrer stood;
The latter seamed tu komprahend
    That trick wood bode no good.

Now tha protest, tha deprykate,
    Tha humble thairselves lo;
Tha wash thair hands in innosens;
    Tha did'nt like the sho.
Their town clark, who'ze as shi at furst,
    And snubbed this stern kommitteigh,
Was abject as a galleigh slave,
    An object ov thair pitty.

The demokrats suggest a klew;
    "Haint gamblers bet upon it?
"And driven to a desperait game,
    "By stelth hav gone and done it!
"But wee — no, tha, the gambling folk
    "Hav done this dubble frawd.
"Us democrats is innosent;
    "Owr parteigh's over slawd!"

And while this blarneigh tauk went on,
    There kame a staulwert throng.
— Republikans they kauld thairselvs —
    Above phive hunderd strong;
And swoar tha voted for thair man,
    And ware identyfide,
And proved thair words by evry test,
    Whatever was applide.

The demokrats a pheint did maik,
    Uv trotten out *thair* men.
When prest — tha prudentleigh with helld,
    For why? the publick ken!
The work of the Kommitteigh dun,
    — Led by the upright Treet —
Back to thair Ledgislative hauls,
    Tha take thair wunted seet.

Deliberatleigh tha make repoart
    Of all the fax, forsuth,
And evereigh onnest man beleaves,
    Tha stated symple truth.
Then Eaton crakt his whip agane
    — Hiz men ar overaud;
Tha roat aganst thair Konshensays, (?)
    To prophet by thair frawd.

But Eton's whip, or Inglish's name
    Skarss brings them into line,
Tha're dancin oar a magazeen,
    While uthers spring the myn
Tha stood the fire of Treet and Hall,
    And Wate, hymnself a hoste,
And knever winst, but new the while,
    That all waz wuss'n lost.

Tha new, that hoo invoak the winds,
    Musst wreep the whurlwind's force;
Thair kowntynanses told the tail
    Of shaim dispare remoss.
Such konstans to thair chozen cheef,
    Belongs to them that win,
But admirashun seeces when,
    We see thair damnin sinn.

Tha strane thairselves to dott an i
    Upon the Constitushun,
But swallough frawd, subvurting all,
    With wunderful degestyan.
Now Inglish's dum, or if he speaks,
    No longer interlardes
Bombastic threts, of kaulling owt
    Mackord or the Hoss Gardz.

The demokratic press dies hard,
    Tho drupid is thair Krest,
Tha phain wood hav poor Inglish write
    The partting woord, "Protestt."
The fether Inglish shows, iz whight,
    Nor wares his black cockaid,
His trenchunt sored is not in site,
    Or sheethid is its blaid.

From orph that Pressidenshull hoss,
    Hee's phell to rize no more.
It yused hiz seet as Gilpinz did,
    For "it haz gauld him sore."
Hiz modest privit clerk cant draw
    That little haff-yeer's pa,
Tho hanging rownd the public krib,
    Has maide him du this way.

Now gentlemen and lobbeyists,
    And politicians tu,
And loryers, (— thoze owtcide the Howse —)
    I have a wurd for yu:
See to what end, by krookid waze,
    Wun parteigh woz led on —
— A parteigh too, whoze vary naim,
    Wunce souwnded like a charme.

An thinke alaz, what tha hadd bin,
    In the braive "daze of yoar,"
Befoar the grate apostasee —
    When Jaxon's knaim tha wore.
Thinke howe tha solde thair principals,
    From tyme to tyme away,
Till tru Republykans hav gaynd,
    The relm tha thru awa.

Twoz Phedrals and Republykans
    In Jeffursun's brite da,
And the latter, if I reed arrite,
    Kept stepp to Freedum's la.
Tha gave to evreigh man hiz rites;
    The slave tha wood sett phree,
And histre sez they'd only wate,
    An oppertunitee.

How Jaxson treeted rebel Staits
    Whare treeson runn so hi!
When Sowth Kerlina razed her flagg,
    And tride to nullyfi!
The Armee and the Navee then,
    Were hurld upon the fo;
Koersion waz the docktrin ov
    Demokracy, I trow.

Or whight or blak, twaz awl the same —
   Old Hickoree, he swore,
That aristockrasee shood not
   Deluge this land with gore.
And then protexyun woz the kri,
   Ov Demokratick lites,
They karrid tu, at thair mast-hed,
   "Free traid and saylers rites."

No inkompatabilitee
   Was found, in daze of yoar,
Betwean *Kummershall* thriftyness,
   And industryse *ashoar*.
Then if the lor woz ever strecht,
   'Twas to pertect the week;
It did'nt hunt poor fugitives,
   And maike a man a sneek.

But late tha tooke the oppressur's rod,
   And woundid freedum soar,
Tha've hunted down poor fugitives,
   And mersee tha ignoar.
Twas vary Konstitutishanall
   To shute a flyin slaiv;
Unkonstitushunall it iz,
   To stopp a Ku Klux nave.

To shelter then theez hounded ones
   Woz treeson, jale, or phine,
And theze dejenerait Demokrats
   Stille phight it on that line.
The flings at sertin kolord Gards,
   The last Eelexyan day,
That same old hunker prejudice,
   Eggs-hibits in phull **pla.**

If the Konstitushunn's nullyfide,
  Bi violens and frawd,
Twould go agin thair konshunses(?)
  To opher a reword.
Awa with sutch vile reesoning,
  Mephistoklees! for shaim!
God nose, the Fundamental Lor,
  Has know subversiv ame!

The parteigh's dedd that praktised it,
  It dyde the other da;
It kild itselph, by nursing frawd,
  It thru itselph awa.
Before it dyde it votid owt,
  (By Aldermen 'tis sayd,)
The hated name "ELECTION," Surs,
  Befoar the word "parade."

Tha tride bi frawd and violense,
  To maike it obseleet,
But failing, tha hav maide that word,
  Thair ghoastlee winding sheat.
Kum to the grave-yard, gentle surs,
  And kindlee dropp a teer,
Upon the Demokratick grave,
  And moysten now thair beer.

Reethe Syprus over Inglish's mound,
  Remmemberr Eatin's urn,
For, whense thave gone, politiklee,
  No travaillers return.
To see ten thowsand folks turn owt,
  Upon electshun da,
Enthiusyasm can not gush,
  From moreners by the way!

Koz why? — it seems fu-nee-ryall,
    To the late partee's friends,
To see a gala da like this,
    With thair own sorrer blends.
How diffrent was that glorius da,
    To the Republikuns!
Who throng and cheer their Govenor,
    The noblest of our suns!

While modist Juel, purist gem!
    The man hoo lurned to wate;
— We onor thee, cheef magistrait!
    Hoo bairs the sored of Stait.
He wares his oners grasefullee,
    His frendshipp's tru and stanch;
And to hiz ennymyes, defunkt,
    Eggstends the ollive braunch.

Harfford Sitteigh, Meigh the Sicksteanth, 1871.

A large broadside, for a copy of which I am indebted to Burney Fishback and the Mark Twain
Research Foundation, Perry, Mo.

THOSE ANNUAL BILLS

[A parody on "Those Evening Bells" by Thomas Moore]

The annual bills! these annual bills!
How many a song their discord trills
Of "truck" consumed, enjoyed, forgot,
Since I was skinned by last year's lot!

Those joyous beans are passed away;
Those onions blithe, O where are they?
Once loved, lost, mourned — *now* vexing ILLS
Your shades troop back in annual bills!

And so 'twill be when I'm aground —
These yearly duns will still go round,
While other bards, with frantic quills,
Shall damn and *damn* these annual bills!

In a letter to James M. Fields, January 7, 1874,
but smoothed into present form before being
printed the following year in *Sketches New and
Old* (Hartford, 1875), 62.

NEW COCK ROBIN

Who's to be Editor of the Tribune?
    I, says Schuyler Colfax!
    Tho' my idle pen doth show lax
    It *can* slaughter like a pole-axe.
    I'm the man to deal in cold facts
    For ten thousand — green or gold backs,
        I'm to be said Editor.

Who's to be Editor of the Tribune?
    I, says Georgius William Curtis!
    What I'm able to assert is
    That as far as rebel dirt is
    Concerned, all clear [*sic*] my shirt is
    I'm the man! And, certes,
    For shares, cash, or seven-thirties,
    My pen that now inert is
    I'll dip in aqua-furtis,*
        Since I'm to be that Editor.

Who's to be Editor of the Tribune?
    I, says Whitelaw Reid!
    On, great Pegasus, my steed,
    I charge the felon Tweed!
    Of all his filthy breed,
    That with a ghoul-like greed
    On our credit's corpse did feed,
    The metropolis I freed.
    Of Reform I took the lead —
    To the West, with ardent speed
    Bent my way. And in the hour of need,
    In Cincinnati sowed the seed
    Of a movement that decreed
    Corruption's death. Alas! the reed —
    Oh, weaker still! — the *weed*
    We leaned on, broke — indeed
    The time was past, I rede,
    For "Liberal" virtue to succeed.

Now I promised naught. I'm keyed
Up to honor's pitch. I'll bleed
Before I'll ever draw a bead
In monopoly's defence. Give heed
To my words. On which basis Whitelaw Reid
     Is content to be that Editor.

Who's to be Editor of the Tribune?
    I, says Speaker Blaine!
Born Republican, I fain —
I! that do scorn to feign
Truth, in forum or in fane —
Would fight, and fight again
Where long, with might and main
I've helped to pile the slain
On Democratic fields, 'mid rain
Of speech and ink, when rebel reign
Seemed imminent and men gave rein
To cowardly impulse and the stain
Of slavish fear wrought bane
In Northern hearts. This brain
Did never yet refrain,
This heart did ne'er complain,
This hand did ne'er disdain
To think, feel, work — unheeding whether gain
Might crown my toil and pain
If I only *could* raise Cain
With that locofoco gang. No grain
Of self doth urge this suit. This strain
Of laudatory song doth drain
The deep fountains of my modesty. O deign
To scan my motive justly. Ah, wane-
ing sun, set fair! And rise on Blaine
     So that I may be that Editor.

Who's to be Editor of the Tribune?
    I, says Mark Twain —
'Tis my Castle in Spain!
I'm the man for the place, though I cannot explain
Why; for the reason that Blaine

The recondite Radical Rep. from Chill Maine
O, bothering, troublesome, itching chil-Blaine —
Has used all the words except vain and insane
That happily rhyme with Yours Truly, Mark Twain.
So I offer no plea — merely pray that the seine
That is dragging for editors the whole inky main
May miss all the whales and catch this sardayne —*
    For I yearn to be that Editor
    Mark Twain

P.S. But failing Colfax, Curtis, Reid, Blaine, Twain
    Thank God there's one Power left — George Francis Train!
    Oh, let old Talk-Talk have a show.

Hartford, Dec. 23 [1872]

* Dismal orthography, but justified by the necessities of poetical composition. M. T.

Sent to Hartford *Evening Post,* copied in Chicago *Tribune,* January 2, 1873. Reprinted in Arthur L. Vogelback, "Mark Twain and the Fight for the *Tribune,*" *American Literature,* XXVI, 377-380 (November, 1954).

KIDITCHIN

O du lieb' Kiditchin
Du bist ganz bewitchin',
    Waw —— he!

In summer days Kiditchin
Thou'rt dear from nose to britchin
    Waw —— he!

No dought thoult get a switchin
When for mischief thou'rt itchin'
    Waw —— he!

But when you're good Kiditchin
You shall feast in James's kitchin
    Waw —— he!

O now lift up thy song —
Thy noble note prolong —
Thou living Chinese gong!
    Waw — he! waw — he waw
    Sweetest donkey man ever saw.

Written 1885, in honor of Jean's donkey
Cadichon, which the girls called Kiditchin. The spelling and punctuation
are those used by Susy in her secret
biography of her father. See Paine's
Biography, 822.

TRANSLATION OF HEINE'S
"DIE LORELEI"

I cannot divine what it meaneth,
This haunting nameless pain:
A tale of the bygone ages
Keeps brooding through my brain:

The faint air cools in the gloaming,
And peaceful flows the Rhine,
The thirsty summits are drinking
The sunset's flooding wine;

The loveliest maiden is sitting
High-throned in yon blue air,
Her golden jewels are shining
She combs her golden hair;

She combs with a comb that is golden,
And sings a weird refrain
That steeps in a deadly enchantment
The list'ner's ravished brain:

The doomed in his drifting shallop,
Is tranced with the sad sweet tone,
He sees not the yawning breakers,
He sees but the maid alone:

The pitiless billows engulf him! —
So perish sailor and bark;
And this, with her baleful singing,
Is the Lorelei's grewsome work.

In Chapter 16 of *A Tramp Abroad*, 1880.

THE DUKE'S VERSION OF HAMLET'S
SOLILOQUY IN *HUCKLEBERRY FINN*

To be or not to be; that is the bare bodkin
That makes calamity of so long life;
For who would fardels bear, till Birnam Wood do come to Dunsinane,
But that the fear of something after death
Murders the innocent sleep,
Great nature's second course,
And makes us rather sling the arrows of outrageous fortune
Than fly to others that we know not of.
There's the respect must give us pause:
Wake Duncan with thy knocking! I would thou couldst;
For who would bear the whips and scorns of time,
The oppressor's wrong, the proud man's contumely,
The law's delay, and the quietus which his pangs might take,
In the dead waste and middle of the night, when churchyards yawn
In customary suits of solemn black,
But that the undiscovered country from whose bourne no traveler returns,
Breathes forth contagion on the world,
And thus the native hue of resolution, like the poor cat i' the adage,
Is sicklied o'er with care,
And all the clouds that lowered o'er our housetops,
With this regard their currents turn awry,
And lose the name of action.
'Tis a consummation devoutly to be wished. But soft you, the fair Ophelia:
Ope not thy ponderous and marble jaws,
But get thee to a nunnery — go!

In Chapter 21 of *Adventures of Huckleberry Finn*, 1885.

ODE TO STEPHEN DOWLING BOTS, DEC'D.

And did young Stephen sicken,
    And did young Stephen die?
And did the sad hearts thicken,
    And did the mourners cry?

No; such was not the fate of
    Young Stephen Dowling Bots;
Though sad hearts round him thickened,
    'Twas not from sickness' shots.

No whooping-cough did rack his frame,
    Nor measles drear, with spots;
Not these impaired the sacred name
    Of Stephen Dowling Bots.

Despised love struck not with woe
    That head of curly knots,
Nor stomach troubles laid him low,
    Young Stephen Dowling Bots.

O no. Then list with tearful eye,
    Whilst I his fate do tell.
His soul did from this cold world fly,
    By falling down a well.

They got him out and emptied him;
    Alas it was too late;
His spirit was gone for to sport aloft
    In the realms of the good and great.

Emmeline Grangerford's poem in Chapter 17
of *Adventures of Huckleberry Finn,* 1885.

MY DOG BURNS

No more shall her beauteous form
Be seen in the raging storm.
No more shall her wondrous tail
Dodge the quickly dropping hail.

She lived a quiet harmless life
In Hartford far from madding strife;
Nor waged no War on peaceful rat
Nor battled with wild fierce tomcat.

No, No, my beloved, dear 'cause dead
What though thy coat was a brick dust red?
Like a good author, thou wast a trusty friend
And thy tail, like his, red to the very end.

Every Other Saturday, I, 457-458 (December 20,
1884). Reprinted in *The Twainian*, p. 3 (July-
August, 1953).

S'KLK! G'LANG!

Mongolfier, as people say,
    With board-bills gaping wide,
Did not repine, nor bow his spine,
Nor wait to dine, or e'en decline:
    But rose and took a ride.

In '92, Columbus true
    The clamorous world decried:
He never winched, he never flinched!
His contract clinched, his belt he cinched,
    Cast off and took a ride.

And Stephenson, bold Stephenson,
    By all misfortune tried,
Sans sword or shield he kept the field
And would not yield. His conquest sealed,
    Ope'd valves and took a ride.

When 'Lijah bold, oppressed of old,
    Saw friends forsake his side,
He didn't walk, he didn't sail,
He didn't squawk, he didn't wail:
    S'klk! G'lang! He took a ride.

L'ENVOI

When troubles loom, and thunders boom
    And darkly rolls YOUR tide,
Don't mope, but smile,
Rouse hope, my child!
    And hail! and take a ride.

Advice to a childhood friend of his
wife's on her marriage, September 1,
1886. First printed in *The Twainian*,
p. 3 (May-June, 1963).

[A PARODY ON SWIFT]

I fade, I faint, I famish, love!
I thirst, I starve —
    Gewhillikins!
And all for my sweet saucy dear —
Her beef, her kisses, pies, & beer
    My Stellakins!

Coley B. Taylor, *Mark Twain's Margins
on Thackeray's "Swift"* (New York,
1935), 46. Swift sometimes called Stella
"Stellakins" and wrote short poems to
her. In the margin Mark Twain wrote,
"Oh, bosh!" and added the lines above.

LOVE SONG

I ask not, "Is thy hope still sure,
Thy love still warm, thy faith secure?"
I ask not, "Dream'st thou still of me? —
Long'st alway to fly to me?" —
    Ah, no — but as the sun includeth all
        The good gifts of the Giver,
    I sum all these in asking thee,
        "O sweetheart, how's your liver?"

For if thy liver worketh right,
Thy faith stands sure, thy hope is bright,
Thy dreams are sweet, and I their god.
Doubt threats in vain — thou scorn'st his rod.
    Keep only thy digestion clear,
    No other foe my love doth fear.

But Indigestion hath the power
To mar the soul's serenest hour —
To crumble adamantine trust,
And turn its certainties to dust —
To dim the eye with nameless grief —
To chill the heart with unbelief —
To banish hope, & faith, & love,
Place heaven below & hell above.
    Then list — details are naught to me
        So thou'st the *sum*-gift of the Giver —
    I ask thee all in asking thee,
        "O darling, how's your liver?"

At a German health resort, 1891-92. Appeared
in the *Medical Fortnightly* (St. Louis), May 15,
1892. Slightly different versions of it are reprinted in *The Twainian*, p. 6 (April, 1944), and
in Neider, ed., *Mark Twain: Life as I Find It*,
231.

THE EARTH INVOKETH THE SUN

(To Livy, November 27, 1892)

If that rich source were not,
    My robes were stripped from me!
    My fields would naked lie,
    My flowers fade and die.
    All bare my world would be,
If that rich source were not.

If that warm ray grew cold,
    My saps would cease in me,
    My dews turn sleet and snow,
    And chill the winds would blow.
    Full drear my world would be
If that sweet sun grew cold.

If that dear light should pale,
    My skies were lost to me! —
    My summits drown'd in night,
    My valleys hid from sight.
    All dark my world would be
If that sweet light should fail.

                    — S. L. C.

See Caroline T. Harnsberger, *Mark Twain: Family Man* (New York, 1960), 53.

THE DERELICT

Almshouse Attendant: "Consider, sir! in a time
long past, the fame of his great services filled the world;
now he lies dying here friendless, forlorn and forgotten,
and mutters his reproaches with unconscious lips."

You sneer, you ships that pass me by,
    Your snow-pure canvas towering proud!
You *traders* base! — why, once such fry
    Paid reverence, when like a cloud
Storm-swept I drove along,
    My Admiral at post, his pennon blue,
Faint in the wilderness of sky, my long
    Yards bristling with my gallant crew,
My ports flung wide, my guns displayed,
    My tall spars hid in bellying sail!
— You struck your topsails then, and made
    Obeisance — *now* your manners fail.

Well, go your way, and let me dream
    Of days long past, when I, like you,
Was strong and young, and life did seem
    Made all for joy; when I, like you,
Did skim the sea all bravely clad,
    And whether skies in splendor shone,
Or palled the world in gloom, was glad:
    O golden days, where are ye flown!

For thirty years I served the wars
    And trod the deep in sinful pride
Begot of my brave battle-scars
    And cherished stains where heroes died.
Remotest oceans knew my fame,
    Remotest lands paid court to me
With thundering guns and spouting flame
    And welcoming hosts on bended knee.

For thirty years. Then came a day
　　When all my pride full low was laid,
And all my honor men did slay
　　As 'twere a worthless thing. They said
"This ship is old, and fails apace;
　　"Her form is warp'd, her spars astrain,
"Her sails but rags — it were disgrace
　　"To let *her* bear the flag again."

The ingrates sold me! and I sank
　　From that high service of the State
To sordid commerce; taking rank
　　With *your* sort; bearing freight
Of hams and soap and corn and hay,
　　And manned by sloven longshore clods
Profaning decks where once held sway
　　The Nelson breed of warrior gods.

Some while I wistful watched to see
　　If my wide world had me forgot:
If fleets would dip their flags to me,
　　And fortresses salute. O lot
Full hard to bear was mine! No soul
　　Remembered me! No topsail strikes,
No color dips! My humble rôle
　　Now 'twas, to dip to these, and strike *my* kites!

Well, thirty years I wrought in trade,
　　And alway shabbier I grew;
And then once more I fell a grade,
　　And carried swine — as freight *and* crew.
Full forty years I bore this cross
　　And led this life of nameless shame,
Then foundered in a happy gale,
　　And derelict became.

The years they come and the years they go,
    As I drift on the lonely sea,
Recking no more than the winds that blow,
    What is in store for me;
For my shames are over, my soul at peace,
    At peace from loathsome strife,
And I wait in patience for my release
    From the insult of this world's life.

Written about 1893. See Jervis Langdon's undated booklet *Samuel Langhorne Clemens,*
published about the centennial year 1935.

THE TALE OF THE YOUNG BLACK CHAP

(Translated from the German)

There came a-walking past the door
A coal-pitch-raven-black young Moor,
The sun it smote him on his smeller,
And so he hoisted his umbrella.
Now came young Ludwig running by,
A-waving, he, his flag on high,
And Kaspar flew to join the band,
His toothsome bretzel in his hand,
While in his wake skips William free,
With hair neat-combed and hoop, you see.
The three they laugh and scoff and wink,
And mock at that poor Missing Link,
Because his skin is black as ink.

Forth stepped the mighty Nicholas, —
Who hates rude ways and slang and sass, —
And brought his ink-stand too, alas!
Says he, "You children list' to me —
Pray let the little stranger be;
He cannot help his sooty hue,
Bleach out at will, be white like you."
But still these urchins, lacking grace,
Did scoff and laugh right in his face,
And laughed yet heartier than before
At that poor pitch-black piteous Moor.

Then Nich'las he did rave and rage —
As per the picture on that page —
And grabb'd those urchins trembling there,
By arm and crop and coat and hair!
Grabb'd William first and Ludwig next,
And Kaspar third (as per the text),
And quicker than the three could wink
He soused them in the turbid ink!
Soused them down with holy spite,
Soused them down with grim delight,
Soused them down clean out of sight.

You see them here, all black as sin —
Much blacker than that Niggerkin —
The Moor a-marching in the light,
The Ink-Blots following dark as night.
Now if they had but hid their glee,
They'd still be white and fair to see.

Berlin, October, 1891. Reprinted in *Slovenly Peter,* translated by Mark Twain (New York, 1935), 18-21. This is one of eleven poems which Mark Twain translated from the German classic by Heinrich Hoffmann.

L'ARBRE FÉE DE BOURLEMONT

Song of the Children

Now what has kept your leaves so green,
    Arbre Fée de Bourlemont?
The children's tears! They brought each grief,
     And you did comfort them and cheer
     Their bruisèd hearts, and steal a tear
       That, healèd, rose a leaf.

And what has built you up so strong,
    Arbre Fée de Bourlemont?
The children's love! They've loved you long:
    Ten hundred years, in sooth,
They've nourished you with praise and song,
And warmed your heart and kept it young —
    A thousand years of youth!

Bide always green in our young hearts,
    Arbre Fée de Bourlemont!
And we shall always youthful be,
    Not heeding Time his flight;
And when, in exile wand'ring, we
Shall fainting yearn for glimpse of thee,
   Oh, rise upon our sight.

In Chapter 2 of *Joan of Arc,* 1895.

CONTRACT WITH MRS. T. K. BEECHER, JULY 2, 1895

If you prove right and I prove wrong,
A million years from now,
In language plain and frank and strong
My error I'll avow
To your dear waking face.

If I prove right, by God His grace,
Full sorry I shall be,
For in that solitude no trace
There'll be of you and me.

A million years, O patient stone,
You've waited for this message.
Deliver it a million hence;
(Survivor pays expressage.)

MARK TWAIN

Written on thin leaves of stone. Appears
in Paine's *Biography*, 1002. First printed
in *Munsey's Magazine*, October, 1895.

[LOVE CAME AT DAWN]

Love came at dawn, when all the world was fair,
When crimson glories, bloom, & song were rife;
Love came at dawn, when hope's wings fanned the air,
And murmured, "I am life."

Love came at even, when the day was done,
When heart & brain were tired & slumber pressed;
Love came at eve, shut out the sinking sun,
And whispered, "I am rest."

MTP, DV #223 (2), © copyright 1966 by the Mark Twain
Company. In a tribute to Susy, 1896. Probably by Mark
Twain.

INVOCATION

Come forth from thy oozy couch,
 O Ornithorhyncus dear!
And greet with a cordial claw
 The stranger that longs to hear

From thy own own [*sic*] lips the tale
 Of thy origin all unknown:
Thy misplaced bone where flesh should be
 And flesh where should be bone;

And fishy fin where should be paw,
 And beaver-trowel tail,
And snout of beast equip'd with teeth
 Where gills ought *to* prevail.

Come, Kangaroo, the good and true!
 Foreshortened as to legs,
And body tapered like a churn,
 And sack marsupial, i'fegs,

And tell us why you linger here,
 Thou relic of a vanished time,
When all your friends as fossils sleep,
 Immortalized in lime!

Written August 22, 1895. This version of the
poem appeared in Chapter 8 of *Following the
Equator,* 1897. In the last stanza I have changed
"tells" to "tell," as it is in the manuscript notebook. In *Mark Twain's Notebook,* 264, Paine
changed line 11 to "And lungs of beast and teeth
of beast," and the final word of the poem to
"rhyme." Both changes violate Mark Twain's
original notebook entry.

A SWELTERING DAY IN AUSTRALIA

(To be read soft and low, with the lights turned down.)

The Bombola faints in the hot Bowral tree,
   Where fierce Mullengudgery's smothering fires
Far from the breezes of Coolgardie
   Burn ghastly and blue as the day expires;

And Murriwillumba complaineth in song
   For the garlanded bowers of Woolloomooloo,
And the Ballarat Fly and the lone Wollongong
   They dream of the gardens of Jamberoo;

The wallabi sighs for the Murrubid*gee,*
   For the velvety sod of the Munno Pa*rah,*
Where the waters of healing from Muloowur*tie*
   Flow dim in the gloaming by Yaranyac*kah;*

The Koppio sorrows for lost Wolloway,
   And sigheth in secret for Murrurun*di,*
The Whangeroo wombat lamenteth the day
   That made him an exile from Jerrilde*rie;*

The Teawamute Tumut from Wirrega's glade,
   The Nangkita swallow, the Wallaroo swan,
They long for the peace of the Timaru shade
   And thy balmy soft airs, O sweet Mittagong!

The Kooringa buffalo pants in the sun,
   The Kondoparinga lies gaping for breath,
The Kongorong Camaum to the shadow has won,
   But the Goomeroo sinks in the slumber of death;

In the weltering hell of the Moorooroo plain
   The Yatala Wangary withers and dies,
And the Worrow Wanilla, demented with pain,
   To the Woolgoolga woodlands despairingly flies;

Sweet Nangwarry's desolate, Coonamble wails,
   And Tungkillo Kuito in sables is drest,
For the Whangerei winds fall asleep in the sails
   And the Booleroo life-breeze is dead in the west.

Mypongo, Kapunda, O slumber no more!
    Yankalilla, Parawirra, be warned!
There's death in the air! Killanoola, wherefore
    Shall the prayer of Penola be scorned?

Cootamundra, and Takee, and Wakatipu,
    Toowoomba, Kaikoura are lost!
From Onkaparinga to far Oamaru
    All burn in this hell's holocaust!

Paramatta and Binnum are gone to their rest
    In the vale of Tapanni Taroom,
Kawakawa, Deniliquin — all that was best
    In the earth are but graves and a tomb!

Narrandera mourns, Cameroo answers not
    When the roll of the scathless we cry:
Tongariro, Goondiwindi, Woolundunga, the spot
    Is mute and forlorn where ye lie.

In Chapter 36 of *Following the Equator,* 1897.

IN MEMORIAM

Olivia Susan Clemens
Died August 18, 1896; Aged 24

In a fair valley — oh, how long ago, how long ago!
Where all the broad expanse was clothed in vines
And fruitful fields and meadows starred with flowers,
And clear streams wandered at their idle will,
And still lakes slept, their burnished surfaces
A dream of painted clouds, and soft airs
Went whispering with odorous breath,
And all was peace — in that fair vale,
Shut from the troubled world, a nameless hamlet drowsed.

Hard by, apart, a temple stood;
And strangers from the outer world
Passing, noted it with tired eyes,
And seeing, saw it not:
A glimpse of its fair form — an answering momentary thrill —
And they passed on, careless and unaware.

They could not know the cunning of its make;
They could not know the secret shut up in its heart;
Only the dwellers of the hamlet knew:
They knew that what seemed brass was gold;
What marble seemed, was ivory;
The glories that enriched the milky surfaces —
The trailing vines, and interwoven flowers,
And tropic birds awing, clothed in tinted fire —
They knew for what they were, not what they seemed:
Encrustings all of gems, not perishable splendors of the brush.
They knew the secret spot where one must stand —
They knew the surest hour, the proper slant of sun —
To gather in, unmarred, undimmed,
The vision of the fane in all its fairy grace,
A fainting dream against the opal sky.
    And more than this. They knew
That in the temple's inmost place a spirit dwelt,
Made all of light!
    For glimpses of it they had caught
Beyond the curtains when the priests
That served the altar came and went.

    All loved that light and held it dear
That had this partial grace;
But the adoring priests alone who lived
By day and night submerged in its immortal glow
Knew all its power and depth, and could appraise the loss
If it should fade and fail and come no more.

    All this was long ago — so long ago!

The light burned on; and they that worship'd it,
And they that caught its flash at intervals and held it dear,
Contented lived in its secure possession. Ah,
How long ago it was!
       And then when they
Were nothing fearing, and God's peace was in the air,
And none was prophesying harm —
The vast disaster fell:
Where stood the temple when the sun went down,
Was vacant desert when it rose again!

    Ah, yes! 'Tis ages since it chanced!

    So long ago it was,
That from the memory of the hamlet-folk the Light has passed —
They scarce believing, now, that once it was,
Or, if believing, yet not missing it,
And reconciled to have it gone.

    Not so the priests! Oh, not so
The stricken ones that served it day and night,
Adoring it, abiding in the healing of its peace:
They stand, yet, where erst they stood
Speechless in that dim morning long ago;
And still they gaze, as then they gazed,
And murmur, "It will come again;
It knows our pain — it knows — it knows —
Ah, surely it will come again."

                                 S. L. C.

LAKE LUCERNE, August 18, 1897.

First printed in *Harper's Magazine*, XCV, 929-930 (November, 1897).

"IN DIM & FITFUL VISIONS
THEY FLIT ACROSS THE DISTANCES"

In Memory of
Olivia Susan Clemens
Departed this life August 18, 1896.

> "I am old, poor lady.
> If sympathy of one whose years ——"

> "*Experience* is age; not years!
> Your face is ignorantly smooth, & ignorantly pink;
> You have lived long, & nothing suffered.
> You try to pity me, I see the good intent, I know it is your best;
> But how shall you pay out in coin
> What yet lies bedded in your ores?
> The fires of grief — *they* lap the heart in flame,
> *They* smelt the red gold free! It is the bleeding heart
> That pays the due of woe in metal fire-assayed, —
> Not kindly-meaning paper
> Drawn upon an unexploited mine
> Which one *may* find some day in case by malice of the fates
> Misfortune shall so order it."

> She dreamed a moment in her past.
> With absent look, & mumbled, in her pain,
> "Oh, I am old in grief — so old!" And presently began
> The story of her wounds, as one who muses to himself,
> Scarce knowing that he speaks:
> "My curly-headed fay!
> My baby girl — how long ago that was! —
> 'Tis five & twenty years — an age!
> "There sat I, thinking of my happiness,
> The riches garnered in my heart, my hopes
> Fulfilled beyond my dreams, & wondering
> If any in the world knew such content as I:
> "And now, from out my veiling lids
> I caught a flash of sun-lit golden hair,
> But kept the secret to myself. I knew the game:

A bear was lurking there, I knew it well,
And knew its ways. All stealthily it crept
In shadow & concealment of the wood —
(Which others thought a sofa of the horse-hair type) —
Until it gained the nearest coign of vantage:
Then — out it burst upon me with a roar, & I
Collapsed in fright! — which was my part to play.

  "O, I can see my darling yet: the little form
In slip of flimsy stuff all creamy white,
Pink-belted waiste with ample bows,
Blue shoes scarce bigger than the house-cat's ears —
Capering in delight & choked with glee
To see me so becrazed with fright.
  "Then suddenly the laughter ceased —
Drowned, dear heart, in penitential tears —
She flew to me & hugged me close,
And kissed my eyes & face & mouth,
And soothed away my fears with anxious words,
'Look up, mama, don't cry; it's not a *real* bear, it's only me.'

  "Ah me, ah me, how could I know
That I should look upon her face no more!"

   "Poor soul! She died? That very day?"

  "No. Lost, I think — or stolen away;
We never knew."

  It smote me cold; it smote me dumb;
There were no words to say. She noted not
Or if I spoke or no, but drifted on
Along her tale of griefs — that weary road
The wretched travel day & night,
From eve to dawn & dawn to eve again,
Whilst happier mortals toil or sleep:
  "No, I have not been spared.
So long ago it seems an age, misfortune comes again.
'Tis sixteen years. Could I forget the count? Ah, no, ah, no.
The dearest little maid — scarce ten years old —
How strange it was — how strange — how strange!

"It was a summer afternoon; the hill
Rose green above me & about, & in the vale below
The distant village slept, & all the world
Was steeped in dreams. Upon me lay this peace,
And I forgot my sorrow in its spell. And now
My little maid passed by, & she
Was deep in thought upon a solemn thing:
A disobedience & my reproof. Upon my face
She "must not look until the day was done;"
For she was doing penance. . . . *She?*
O, it was *I!* What mother knows not that?
And so she passed. I worshiping & longing. . . .
It was not wrong? You do not think me wrong?
I did it for the best. Indeed I meant it so.
And it was done in love — not passion; no,
But only love. You do not think me wrong?
'Twould comfort me to think I was not wrong. . . .
If I had spoken! If I had known — if I had only known!

  "As then she was, I see her still;
And ever as I look, awake or in my dreams,
She passes by. Unheeding me, she passes by!
  "By duty urged, I checked the hail all charged with love
That burned upon my tongue, & let her pass unwelcomed —
Sat worshiping, & let her pass unwelcomed. . . .
Ah, how was I to know that doom was in the air!

  "She flits before me now:
The peach-bloom gown of gauzy crêpe,
The plaited tails of hair,
The ribbons floating from the summer hat,
The grieving face, droop'd head absorbed with care.
O, dainty little form! —
I see it move, receding slow along the path,
By hovering butterflies besiged [*sic*]; I see it reach
The breezy top & show clear-cut against the sky. . . .
Then pass beyond & sink from sight — forever!"

  "To death?"

"God knows. But lost to me;
To come no more, to bless my eyes no more in life.
Where now she wanders — if she wander still & live —
That shall I never know. . . . And there is yet
Another."

"Gone?"

"Taken while I stood & gazed!"

"O, pitiful!"

"In presence of a hundred friends
She vanished from my eyes! In my own house
It was. Within, was light & cheer; without,
A blustering winter's night. There was a play;
It was her own; for she had wrought it out,
Unhelped, from her own head — & she
But turned sixteen! A pretty play,
All graced with cunning fantasies,
And happy songs, & peopled all with fays,
And sylvan gods & goddesses,
And shepherds, too, that piped & danced,
And wore the guileless hours away
In care-free romps & games.
      "Her girlhood mates played in the piece,
And she as well: a goddess, she, —
And looked it, as it seemed to me.
      " 'Twas fairyland restored — so beautiful it was
And innocent. It made us cry, we elder ones,
To live our lost youth o'er again
With these its happy heirs.
      "Slowly, at last, the curtain fell.
Before us, there, she stood, all wreathed & draped
In roses pearled with dew — so sweet, so glad,
So radiant! — and flung us kisses through the storm
Of praise that crowned her triumph. . . . O,
Across the mists of time I see her yet,
My Goddess of the Flowers!

. . . . "The curtain hid her. . . .
Do you comprehend? Till time shall end!
Out of my life she vanished while I looked!

. . . . "Ten years are flown.
O, I have watched so long,
Life lost its worth. And when the blank was past,
And we drank life again from out each other's eyes
And lips & speech — oh, heaven itself could nothing add
To that contenting joy! . . .

"I would you could have seen her.
If you, a stranger . . . But you will never see her now;
Nor I — oh, never more!

. . . . "How beautiful she was!
Not outwardly alone, — within, as well. Her spirit
Answered to her face, her mind ennobled both. . . .
And now. . . .
O, now to know that in that wonder-working intellect
The light is quenched, the cunning wheels are still,
The eyes that spoke, the voice that charmed,
Have ceased from their enchantments!

. . . . "How dear she was! how full of life!
A creature made of joyous fire & flame & impulse —
A living ecstasy! Ah who could dream
That she could die? . . . Two years — two little years ago. . . .
"It seems so strange. . . . so strange . . .
Struck down unwarned!
In the unbought grace of youth laid low —
In the glory of her fresh young bloom laid low —
In the morning of her life cut down!
"And I not by! Not by
So long. But she will come no more. . . .
No more. No, she will come no more."

She sobbed, & dumbly moaned, a little time,
I, silent, wanting words to comfort griefs like these;
Then, sighing, took she up her tale again:

"Yet even this I over-lived,
And in my heart of hearts gave thanks
That of my jewels one was left,
That of my jewels still the richest one
Was spared me to delight my eye
And light the darkness of my days.
   "My idol, she!
I hugged her to my dreading soul — my precious one! —
And daily died with fear. For now,
To me all things were terrors, that before
Were innocent of harm: the rain, the snow, the sun —
I blenched if they but touched her.
   "O, tall & fair & beautiful she was!
And all the world to me, & I to her. In her I lived,
And she in me. We were not two, but one.
And it was little like the common tie that binds
The mother & the child, but liker that
Which binds two lovers:
The hours were blank when we were separate;
The time was heavy & the sun was cold,
When the shadows fell, the night of death closed down,
The sun that lit my life went out. Not by to answer
When the latest whisper passed the lips
That were so dear to me — my name!
Far from my post! the world's whole breadth away.
O, sinking in the waves of death she cried to me
For mother-help, & got for answer —
Silence!"

              "O, you wring my heart!
God pity you, poor lady! God pity you, & grant
That this hard stroke shall be the last
That in His providence —"
   I stopped — rebuked by something in her face.
She drifted into dreams — she did not hear;
Her thoughts were far away,
Wandering among the ruins of her life.
Then presently she muttered to herself,
          "All gone.

All; & she, the last, my joy, my pride, my solace —
Dead. Dead, in the perfected flower of her youth."

She rose, & went her way.
I questioned one who seemed to know her, & he said,
 "Poor lady, she is mad.
She is bereft of four, she thinks. There was but one."

Ah, God!
And yet, poor broken heart, she said the truth!
We that are old — we comprehend; even we
That are not mad: whose grown-up scions still abide,
Their tale complete:
Their earlier selves we glimpse at intervals
Far in the dimming past;
We see the little forms as once they were,
And whilst we ache to take them to our hearts,
The vision fades. We know them lost to us —
Forever lost; we cannot have them back;
We miss them as we miss the dead,
We mourn them as we mourn the dead.

S. L. C.

York Harbor, August 18, 1902.

MTP, DV #220, © copyright 1966 by the Mark Twain Company, and printed here in its entirety for the first time. This is a neat eleven-page AMS, with only half a dozen slight revisions. Apparently the poem was written at one sitting. Paine quotes 86 lines in Appendix U of the *Biography*, taking certain liberties with the AMS, as does also the typescript in MTP, DV #220a (Paine #61).

TO THE ABOVE OLD PEOPLE

Sleep! for the Sun that scores another Day
Against the Tale allotted You to stay,
  Reminding You, is Risen, and now
Serves Notice — ah, ignore it while You may!

The chill Wind blew, and those who stood before
The Tavern murmured, "Having drunk his Score,
  Why tarries He with empty Cup? Behold,
The Wine of Youth once poured, is poured no more.

"Come leave the Cup, and on the Winter's Snow
Your Summer Garment of Enjoyment throw:
  Your Tide of Life is ebbing fast, and it,
Exhausted once, for You no more shall flow."

While yet the Phantom of false Youth was mine,
I heard a Voice from out the Darkness whine,
  "O Youth, O whither gone? Return,
And bathe my Age in thy reviving Wine."

In this subduing Draught of tender green
And kindly Absinthe, with its wimpling Sheen
  Of dusky half-lights, let me drown
The haunting Pathos of the Might-Have-Been.

For every nickled Joy, marred and brief,
We pay some day its Weight in golden Grief
  Mined from our Hearts. Ah, murmur not —
From this one-sided Bargain dream of no Relief!

The Joy of Life, that streaming through their Veins
Tumultuous swept, falls slack — and wanes
  The Glory in the Eye — and one by one
Life's Pleasures perish and make place for Pains.

Whether one hide in some secluded Nook —
Whether at Liverpool or Sandy Hook —
  'Tis one. Old Age will search him out — and He —
He — He — when ready will know where to look.

From Cradle unto Grave I keep a House
Of Entertainment where may drowse
    Bacilli and kindred Germs — or feed — or breed
Their festering Species in a deep Carouse.

Think — in this battered Caravanserai,
Whose Portals open stand all Night and Day,
    How Microbe after Microbe with his Pomp
Arrives unasked, and comes to stay.

Our ivory Teeth, confessing to the Lust
Of masticating, once, now own Disgust
    Of Clay-plug'd Cavities — full soon our Snags
Are emptied, and our Mouths are filled with Dust.

Our Gums forsake the Teeth and tender grow,
And fat, like over-ripened Figs — we know
    The Sign — the Riggs Disease is ours, and we
Must list this Sorrow, add another Woe.

Our Lungs begin to fail and soon we Cough,
And chilly Streaks play up our Backs, and off
    Our fever'd Foreheads drips an icy Sweat —
We scoffed before, but now we may not scoff.

Some for the Bunions that afflict us prate
Of Plasters unsurpassable, and hate
    To cut a Corn — ah cut, and let the Plaster go,
Nor murmur if the Solace come too late.

Some for the Honors of Old Age, and some
Long for its Respite from the Hum
    And Clash of sordid Strife — O Fools,
The Past should teach them what's to Come:

Lo, for the Honors, cold Neglect instead!
For Respite, disputatious Heirs a Bed
    Of Thorns for them will furnish. Go,
Seek not Here for Peace — but Yonder — with the Dead.

For whether Zal and Rustam heed this Sign,
And even smitten thus, will not repine,
    Let Zal and Rustam shuffle as they may,
The Fine once levied they must Cash the Fine.

O Voices of the Long Ago that were so dear!
Fall'n Silent, now, for many a Mould'ring Year,
    O whither are ye flown? Come back,
And break my Heart, but bless my grieving Ear.

Some happy Day my Voice will Silent fall,
And answer not when some that love it call:
    Be glad for Me when this you note — and think
I've found the Voices lost, beyond the Pall.

So let me grateful drain the Magic Bowl
That medicines hurt Minds and on the Soul
    The Healing of its Peace doth lay — if then
Death claim me — Welcome be his Dole!

SANNA, SWEDEN, September 15th. [1899]

First printed in *McClure's Magazine,* January, 1900.
Also in Works, XXIII, 259-261.

APOSTROPHE TO DEATH

Dublin, N.H.
June 26/05.

O thou, the only kind & dear, the only generous!
Sole of all the gods of all the heavens
That dost not keep a trader's shop & peddle benefits!
Saying to such & such an one, "Believe,
And thou shalt have a profit;" to this,
"Art lame & blind? be healed! — *& pay the price;*"
To these, "Ye've sinned, & would forgiveness have?
Then pay the market rate, a contrite spirit & a broken heart —
We nothing furnish gratis here;"
To this wan mother, "How? the child escaped
Unreconciled, & fries in hell for Adam's sin
And thy neglect, & thou hast come a-begging in the child's behoof?
Ten billion years of fire & flame! — the terms are cheap;
Be grateful, thou, & go thy way. · · · And yet, be comforted, poor soul,
For thou shalt sit aloft in comradeship with souls redeemed
By bargain-counter trade, cash-paid in unoffending blood,
And look upon the little creature's agony
And salve thy grief with soft philosophies that teach
How sweet it is to kiss the rod that smites."

Ah, that shop! One fetid blast of adulation
Lifted up with life's last breath from out a sinner's rotten soul
Can buy free quarters in the house not made with hands;
One luckless sin pain-wrung from out the whitest soul
At such a time, damns it to lodging with the child!

Thou sorry shop! thou sordid Trust!
Consolidated Gas translated to the skies!
With light for all — at Dingley-tariff rates;
With gratis light for none; with lying cooked reports
Proclaiming business done sans money & sans price —
Accept these flatteries, & set them to a song
And give them to that mother & the rest to sing.

O Death, the only kind & dear & generous!
Sole of all the gods of all the heavens
That dost not keep a trader's shop & peddle benefits;
Whose unbought mercy is for all alike; whose pity & whose peace
Go free to all, unsmirched by bargain-taint;
Whose gentle refuge standeth wide
To all that weary are: the soiled, the pure,
The rich, the poor, the unloved & the loved!
Who barreth none; who saith to all,
"My peace I *give* to thee" — not sell!
"Enter thou in, & rest."
    O Death, O sweet & gracious friend,
I bare my smitten head to Thee, & at thy sacred feet
I set my life's extinguished lamp & lay my bruisèd heart.
      I worship thee, & thee alone;
I lay my bruisèd heart. I worship thee, & thee alone;
Would kneel to thee, were't meet to offer, where one loves,
The attitude that shames both him that kneels & him that suffers it.

MTP, Paine #122, printed here for the first time, © copyright 1966 by the Mark Twain Company. There is a rough draft of this poem also, but the clean AMS has only five or six minor revisions.

BATTLE HYMN OF THE REPUBLIC

(Brought down to date)

Mine eyes have seen the orgy of the launching of the Sword;
He is searching out the hoardings where the stranger's wealth is stored;
He hath loosed his fateful lightnings, and with woe and death has scored;
    His lust is marching on.

I have seen him in the watch-fires of a hundred circling camps,
They have builded him an altar in the Eastern dews and damps;
I have read his doomful mission by the dim and flaring lamps —
    His night is marching on.

I have read his bandit gospel writ in burnished rows of steel:
"As ye deal with my pretensions, so with you my wrath shall deal;
Let the faithless son of Freedom crush the patriot with his heel;
    Lo, Greed is marching on!"

We have legalized the strumpet and are guarding her retreat;*
Greed is seeking out commercial souls before his judgment seat;
O, be swift, ye clods, to answer him! be jubilant, my feet!
    Our god is marching on!

In a sordid slime harmonious, Greed was born in yonder ditch,
With a longing in his bosom — and for others' goods an itch —
As Christ died to make men holy, let men die to make us rich —
    Our god is marching on.

* In Manila the Government has placed a certain industry under the protection
of our flag. [Mark Twain's note.]

Probably written about 1901. Printed in Philip S. Foner, *Mark Twain: Social
Critic* (New York, 1958), 278. I have corrected several errors in Foner, such
as restoring "night" for "might" in stanza 2, "O" for "Or" in stanza 4, "others' "
for "other's" in stanza 5. I also put back the quotation marks in stanza 3 and
the "As" in stanza 5.

MY LAST THOUGHT

    I meant my country well —
God is my witness, this is true. In the beginning
I did not waver in my trust, but gave her loyal service —
The fair and just, when they reflect, will grant me this.
They know I was not bad at heart,
Though now they think my heart has changed. . . .
And so it has — but not as *they* conceive! They think
It black & hard — whereas it only bleeds! Bleeds
For the widows it has made, the orphans it has starved,
The freedom it has crushed, the humble friends
It turned against, the faiths it broke,
The treacheries it devised, the freed slaves
It chained again,
The land it took by fraud & keeps by force,
The praise it won from sceptred thieves
For stooping to their ways,
The dirt it put upon our flag & name!

    Lord God, forgive! For I was only weak,
Not bad. And I was out of place —
A lost & wandering atom in that vast Seat
Which only Lincolns & their like compactly fill.
I loved my country, & I meant it well:
I say it with my dying breath. . . . .
    Pearl of the Antilles, speak!
I broke your chains, I set you free; I raised
My country's honor to the skies; I won
The Old World's scorn & hate, the New World's
"Well done, thou faithful son!"

    O *then* I was myself! Grant me that!
Remember only that, dear land of my nativity,
Which I have brought to shame — forget the rest!
I erred through weakness, not intent. For I
Was overborne by sordid counsels,
Base ambitions, & from my head I took

The precious laurel I had earned, & in its place
I set this poor tin glory, now my wear,
Of World-Power, Conqueror of helpless tribes,
Extinguisher of struggling liberties!

Forget? Thou? No — that is a dream.
Thou canst not. The memory of treasons such as mine
Remains. They make a bartered nation blush;
And the wise know that only deeds
That lift a people's pride, & deeds
That make it hang its head,
Abide forever in its heart.

Arnold! How they crimson at his name! And yet —
Why, *his* meditated treason but concerned a garrison —
Mine — accomplished — peddled out a Nation & its honor:
And sold them for a song!

Upon my fading sight a holy vision rises:
Our Flag of snow & flame far-flashing in the sky!
And toward it the oppressed of every clime
Uplifting their poor fettered hands
In hope & trust & worship. . . . .

It is gone. . . . . How blest am I
That the last office of my dying eyes should be
To show it me as once it was: protector of the wronged,
Defender of the weak, friend of the homeless & forlorn!

. . . . But there! — is not this the Flag again?
The dimness grows. It is the Flag, I think, but changed. . . .
The twilight mellows. . . . .
Now the picture clears. . . . It is the Flag, but —
O, not as it was in its great old days!
The Stars are gone, a Skull & Bones
Are in their place; the Red Bars are there,
But soaked with guiltless blood;
The White Bars are Black —
Hide it from my sight!

The night of Death is come:
Its shadows deepen — let me sleep. . . .
Sleep & forget, sleep and be forgotten —
If that dear boon might but be mine!
    Farewell, my Country —
So beloved of me, & so betrayed! I have sinned,
And I repent — have charity!
    Teach the flowers that spring where I am hid,
And wandering summer airs that blow above my grave,
To speak for my dumb lips
And say to any that would search me out, "Pass on —
Naught can ye learn of him:
Give him of your peace, forgive him & forget —
Pass on!"

New York, May, 1901

This is a neat nine-page ink AMS in MTP, Paine #6.
It contains only four slight revisions. The poem is
printed here for the first time, © copyright 1966 by
the Mark Twain Company. The poem is complete, the
series of dots being Mark Twain's own punctuation.

[GOODNIGHT, SWEETHEART, GOODNIGHT]

Goodnight, Sweetheart, goodnight —
The stars are shining bright,
The snow is turning white,
Dim is the failing light,
Fast falls the glooming night, —
    All right!
    Sleep tight!
    Goodnight.

Written February, 1904, when Livy
was on her deathbed in Florence and
Mark Twain was not allowed to visit
her. In Clara Clemens, *My Father:
Mark Twain* (New York, 1931), 248.

POEM TO MARGARET

Be good, be good, be always good,
    And now and then be clever,
But don't you ever be *too* good,
    Nor ever be too clever;

For each as be too awful good
    The awful lonely are,
And such as often clever be
    Get cut and stung and trodden on by persons of lesser mental capac-
ity . . . [for several more lines, ending with the note:] (It is best not to go
on; I think the line is already longer than it ought to be for true poetry.)

Probably written about 1907 for one of the favorite little girls in his club
which he called the Aquarium. In the *Mark Twain Quarterly*, V, 23 (Summer,
1942).

CUSHION FIRST

When all your days are dark with doubt,
    And dying hope is at its worst;
When all life's balls are scattered wide,
With not a shot in sight, to left or right,
Don't give it up;
Advance your cue and shut your eyes,
    And take the cushion first.

Paine, *Biography*, 1407, says that on his return
from England in 1907, Mark Twain felt inspired to write these lines about his favorite
billiard shot.